INSIGHT GU Eastern   May 2014

EXPLORE

ISTANBUL

D1279498

CONTENTS

ANCIENT REMAINS

Explore the city's Roman and Byzantine heritage at the Museum of Archaeology (route 3), followed by the awe-inspiring Hagia Sophia (route 1), the Theodosian Walls and the Kariye Museum (route 11).

RECOMMENDED ROUTES FOR...

ESCAPING THE CROWDS

Take time out at the Pierre Loti Teahouse in Eyüp (route 13), stroll the peaceful streets of Fener and Balat (route 12) or potter around the mosques of Üsküdar (route 14).

NIGHT OWLS

For good times after dark, head for the bohemian bars of Tünel (route 6), or step up the pace at the high-octane clubs near Taksim Square (route 7) or by the Bosphorus (route 8).

OTTOMAN ATMOSPHERE

Admire the masterpieces of Sinan, the greatest Ottoman architect, such as the Süleymaniye Mosque (route 10) and the Rüstem Paşa Mosque in Eminönü (route 5). Be sure to stop by the Topkapı Palace too (route 3).

PAMPERING

Relax after a busy day of sightseeing with a long hot soak, a brisk rub down and an oil massage at Çemberlitaş Hamam (route 1).

SHOPAHOLICS

Haggle your heart out in the Grand Bazaar (route 4) or quietly browse the Arasta and Egyptian bazaars (route 2 and route 5). Check out İstiklal Caddesi for high-street fashions or Çukurcuma for antiques (both route 7).

SPIRITUAL SUSTENANCE

Watch the Sufi mystics whirl away at the Galata Dervish Lodge (route 6), take refuge in the quiet Şehzade Mosque (route 10) or join the devout at the Muslim pilgrimage site of Eyüp (route 13).

VILLAGE LIFE

Experience another side of İstanbul life in the tranquil Bosphorus villages of Ortaköy (route 8), Arnavutköy and Rumeli Hisarı (route 9), or float past them on a boat trip along the Bosphorus (route 15).

INTRODUCTION

An introduction to Istanbul's geography, customs and culture, plus illuminating background information on cuisine, history and what to do when you're there.

Hagia Sophia mosque

EXPLORE ISTANBUL

The gateway to Asia, İstanbul is Europe's largest and most exotic city. Containing remnants of the Roman, Byzantine and Ottoman empires, the city mixes centuries–old mosques and bazaars with air–conditioned shopping malls.

'If one had but a single glance to give the world, one should gaze on İstanbul', wrote the French statesman and poet Alphonse de Lamartine after a visit to the city in 1833. He was one of many 19th-century Western travellers beguiled by İstanbul's intriguing oriental culture, magical architecture and sublime natural topography of undulating hills cut through by the sparkling blue Bosphorus (Boğaziçi).

Lamartine was not the first and by no means the last to be taken by this city poised on Europe's far eastern and Asia's far western edges. Hotly fought over for centuries by various invading forces, it's the only city in the world that has been the capital of both a Christian and an Islamic empire.

Here, where the Black Sea blends into the Aegean, East and West mingle and merge in the cultural melting pot of Turkey's largest metropolis. There are busy oriental bazaars, towering malls and designer-fashion boutiques; traditional kebab shops and *meyhanes* (*meze* and fish taverns) sit alongside chic bars and nightclubs; offices and hotels alternate with Ottoman minarets along the city's skyline.

CITY LAYOUT

İstanbul owes its long-held historical significance to a strategic location at the mouth of the Bosphorus. From this vantage point the city could control not only the ships that passed through the strait on the important trade route between the Black Sea and the Mediterranean, but also the overland traffic crossing from Europe in to Asia Minor.

The western, European half of the city is divided into two by the Golden Horn (Haliç). This estuary forms a natural harbour that separates the old walled city of Constantinople to the south and the modern centre of Beyoğlu to the north.

İstanbul's historical attractions are concentrated in the Sultanahmet area of the Old City, and are easily explored on foot. A handy option for crossing the Golden Horn is to catch the tram from Sultanahmet to Kabataş ferry port, northeast of Beyoğlu. Alternatively, you can walk across the Galata Bridge.

Ferries, buses and *dolmuşes* (minivans) also help to lighten the congested city streets, as well as a couple of funicular railways that ease the ascent of the steep hills of Beyoğlu.

Looking across to Beyoğlu from the Asian shore

HISTORY AND ARCHITECTURE

Three great civilisations have shaped the heart of Old İstanbul – Roman, Byzantine and Ottoman. Although little remains from Roman times, the city's Byzantine legacy boasts Hagia Sophia (the Church of the Divine Wisdom), one of the world's greatest sacred buildings; the magnificent mosaics of St Saviour in Chora (now the Kariye Museum); and the impressive Theodosian Walls. The Ottomans built countless mosques in their capital, the finest of which is the Süleymaniye, built by Turkey's finest architect, Sinan. But the most popular tourist sight is Topkapı Palace, home of the Ottoman sultans, where the riches of the Imperial Treasury and the intrigue of the Harem draw many thousands of visitors each year.

Istanbul has a young population

CLIMATE

İstanbul is subject to a temperate climate, with cool, wet winters and warm, dry summers. For mild conditions that lend themselves to extensive walking, the best time to visit is from April to June, or in September and October.

If you don't mind the heat and humidity, however, it's worth noting that the city really comes alive during the summer months, with the opening of rooftop cafés and restaurants as well as the famous Bosphorus clubs. The ample bodies of water that surround the city usually ensure that the summer heat is tempered by a sea breeze, while also providing plenty of options for sailing and bathing, especially around the Princes' Islands.

December to February can be as cold as anywhere in northern Europe. During this time there's always a chance of snow, which tends to cripple the city's infrastructure, but can also show the domes and minarets of İstanbul at their most beautiful.

POPULATION

With an estimated population of over 13.8 million – an increase of over 1,000 per cent in the last century – İstanbul has seen a boom in its inhabitants since the foundation of the Republic in 1923.

The wide reach of the Ottoman territories, whose boundaries once stretched from Persia through the Arabian

Fishermen on Galata Bridge

Peninsula as far as Vienna, ensured that communities from all over the region came to settle in the empire's capital city. As well as the large Greek populace that was already resident in the region, these included Jews, Armenians, Russians, Kurds and immigrants from the Balkans, all of whom can still be seen living in the city, making up the 25 per cent of İstanbul's non-ethnic Turks. The majority of immigrants who moved here from the mid-1980s onwards originally settled in *gecekondus*, properties that were thrown up overnight with no thought for aesthetics. Slowly the government

DON'T LEAVE ISTANBUL WITHOUT...

Shopping in the Grand Bazaar. When it comes to shopping in İstanbul, all roads lead to the Grand Bazaar, a mash-up of shops selling everything from garish gold bracelets intended as wedding presents to copper lamps, carpets and luxurious fabrics perfect for the maximalist bedroom. See page 44.

Checking out some Byzantine splendour. The glory that was Byzantium hangs on today in the glittering mosaics of Hagia Sophia and the Kariye Museum, the most obvious relics of the splendid past. See pages 30 and 80.

Soaking up some Ottoman atmosphere. To get a feel for Ottomania, you really have to start your explorations in the Topkapı Palace, sizing up the kaftans of the sultans, gazing at the egg-sized emeralds and admiring the cool, tiled bedrooms of the Harem. See page 38.

Indulging in romance. Make a dinner reservation at one of the Bosphorus fish restaurants where the waiters are expert at making their guests feel special, or take the cable car to the Pierre Loti Teahouse in Eyüp and savour a view that once captivated a true French romantic. See pages 71 and 87.

Being pampered. With their hamams (Turkish baths), the Turks were into pampering long before the modern vogue for self-indulgence. Today, you can still have a massage in the Cağaloğlu Hamam, the bath where Florence Nightingale soaped away the stresses of treating the injured from the Crimean battlefield. Or head for the Süleymaniye Hamam which offers mixed bathing in an achingly historic building. See pages 23 and 77.

Having a night on the town. When it comes to lively nightlife, head to Beyoğlu when the sun goes down to party at Ghetto or Indigo. After something a little more olde worlde? Then you could always prop up the bar in the famous Pera Palace Hotel, redolent of the era of the Orient Express. See pages 120 and 55.

Having dinner with a view. In a city renowned for its spectacular views, landing a table for dinner that lets you enjoy good food while gazing out over the Bosphorus, Sea of Marmara or Golden Horn has to be the ultimate goal.

Whirling Dervishes

Muslims at prayer in Eyüp

is rehousing people in high-rise blocks on the outskirts of town which is pushing ever further outwards into Thrace (Europe) and Anatolia (Asia). Most visitors barely glimpse these rather depressing Soviet-style developments although they form a big part of modern İstanbul.

With the exception of the small Orthodox Christian, Armenian and Jewish communities, the vast majority of residents are Muslims, with some neighbourhoods, such as Fatih and Eyüp, adhering more noticeably to Islamic codes of behaviour and dress than others.

Local customs

The rhythm of daily life is entirely dependent on the neighbourhood in İstanbul. If visiting Fatih, Eyüp or any mosques in the city, it is advisable for both men and women to dress moderately, covering their arms and legs, and for women to cover their heads when entering a mosque. In Beyoğlu and along the Bosphorus, however, the dress code is more in tune with other Western cities. These areas are also best for nightlife, as the older parts of the city, like Sultanahmet and Eminönü, tend to shut down after dark.

POLITICS

Turkey is a secular republic that broke from its Ottoman heritage in the 1920s, led by the Republic's much-revered founder Mustafa Kemal Atatürk.

During his time in power, he introduced a host of reforms to bring the country in line with Western practice. Atatürk's image is still ubiquitous in İstanbul, and his persona is held in high esteem. Defaming his memory, the national flag or indeed the very concept of Turkishness that he built into the constitution are considered serious crimes in Turkey.

Secularism and religion

The secularist infrastructure that Atatürk installed survives more or less untouched to this day. But not all Turks agree with having religion so far separated from the state, and many conflicts have arisen in ideological arenas, such as the issue of wearing headscarves in universities and public institutions. Indeed, the Islamic-leaning Justice and

Turks love tea

Detail of the New Mosque's courtyard, Eminönü

Development Party, the AKP, has been in power since 2002, under the leadership of Prime Minister Recep Tayyip Erdoğan and President Abdullah Gül. Nevertheless, the military remains on hand to safeguard Atatürk's legacy from any militant Islamic forces. The dichotomy of secularism and religion is likely to remain on the agenda for some time yet, as the government works toward membership of the EU.

Beginning in May 2013, protests raised against the plans of replacing Taksim Gezi Park with a shopping mall and possible residence developed into riots in Taksim Square when a group occupying the park was attacked by police. Hundreds were arrested and thousands injured. The subject of the protests has since broadened beyond the development of Taksim Gezi Park to include issues such as freedom of assembly and freedom of expression, as well as more broadly defending the secularism of Turkey.

Economics

After a period of massive growth from 2003, Turkey's economy began to contract in early 2008, a situation worsened by the global financial crisis in the autumn of that year. However, since then the country has been affected far less than elsewhere in Europe. An upshot for Western tourists has been the favourable exchange rates with the dollar, pound and euro, although to compensate, most tourist markets are raising prices.

CULTURAL CAPITAL

For those expecting an orientalist time warp, the first impression of Turkey, with Istanbul as a particularly animated gateway, is perhaps something of a surprise. One legacy of Atatürk that had a huge impact on İstanbul was the relocation of the nation's capital to Ankara. Thus İstanbul was freed of its political function, allowing it the space to develop into the rich and diverse cultural capital we see today, highlighted in its role as European Capital of Culture in 2010.

Ramazan

If you happen to visit İstanbul during the holy month of Ramazan, you will notice a few changes in the daily life of the city. Many residents of İstanbul observe the *oruç* (fast) during this period, which means that they don't eat, drink or smoke from sunrise to sunset (although it is safe to assume that most restaurants in this very secular city will stay open all day). *Iftar*, the breaking of the fast, often happens in public places, especially just outside mosques and in big tents erected by the local municipality, where food is distributed to anyone willing to wait in line. In 2014 Ramazan will take place between 28 June and 27 July, while in 2015 it is set to fall between 17 June and 16 July.

Tomb enclosure at Fatih Mosque

TOP TIPS FOR EXPLORING ISTANBUL

What not to eat. Standards of hygiene in cafés and restaurants are generally very good, although it is worth trusting your instinct about a place. Caution should be exercised in the summer, especially if you suspect the street vendors' stuffed mussels and *çiğ köfte* (raw lamb meatballs) might have spent too long in the sun. Do not drink tap water – none of the locals do.

Tax back. Visitors to Turkey are eligible for an 18 percent tax refund on purchases over 100YTL in any one participating store. Look out for the blue Tax Free Shopping sign and ask for your Global Refund Cheques at the counter. On leaving Turkey, find the customs office at the airport before you check in, and present your goods with the relevant receipts and forms.

Underground sound. The fabulous acoustics of the Basilica Cistern make it a perfect performing venue, especially for occasional classical music concerts. Enquire at the ticket desk for the schedule.

Carpet auction. For a taste of the old bazaar of the Orient, head to the Sandal Bedesteni on a Wednesday to witness the chaotic weekly carpet and rug auction. Wares range from silk Persian rugs to Anatolian prayer rugs.

Funicular. If you don't fancy the haul up the hill from the Galata Bridge to Tünel, then hop aboard the funicular on Tersane Caddesi and ascend in style. Built in 1875, it is the second-oldest underground train in the world (after the London Underground), and it meets up in Tünel Square with another antique form of transport, the 19th-century İstiklal Caddesi tram.

Labels for less. Bargain-hunters should head for the hidden passageways off İstiklal Caddesi, where the stalls are overflowing with factory seconds from major US and UK high-street brands manufactured in Turkey. Check out the Beyoğlu İş Merkezi (İstiklal Caddesi 187) with its four subterranean floors of clothing.

İstanbul Biennial. Come in the autumn of an odd year (eg 2015), and be caught up in the wave of art fever that sweeps the city during the İstanbul Biennial. Contemporary art exhibitions crop up during this two-month period (usually mid-Sept–mid-Nov), with İstanbul Modern providing the main venue. Find out more at www.iksv.org/bienal.

Bosphorus clubs. Head to one of İstanbul's Bosphorus nightclubs, famed for open-air opulence and fashionista clientele. If you are visiting in summer, be sure to go – just remember to reserve in advance and that it's easier to get in on weekday nights.

Ahrida Synagogue. Due to increased security risks, the city's synagogues are no longer open to the public. However, if you wish to enter the Ahrida complex (or any other synagogue), you can apply to the Chief Rabbi by filling out the online request at www.turkyahudileri.com.

Turkish Delight

FOOD AND DRINK

Although it's customary for Turks to venerate their mother's cooking, there is none-theless a mouth-watering array of choices for eating out. From seafood to Ottoman feasts to Turkish-international fusion, İstanbul's larder is packed with goodies.

Far more than just the modest kebab, Turkish cuisine is a colourful amalgam of centuries-old traditional Anatolian cooking and sumptuous Ottoman recipes, with influences from Turkey's Arab, Mediterranean and Balkan neighbours. This combination of styles makes for a diverse cuisine that ranges from the vibrant delicacies of vast *meze* trays to grilled meats and fish, from soups and stews to delectable desserts.

If you fancy a break from Turkish cuisine, there are plenty of other options to be found. Beyoğlu boasts a large number of international restaurants: Thai, Japanese, Russian, Georgian, French and Italian eateries can all be found dotted along the streets that branch off the main drag, İstiklal Caddesi. In addition, there are numerous cafés that serve up dependable staples like sandwiches, salads, pasta and hamburgers.

WHERE TO EAT

If you are staying in Sultanahmet, head for the cluster of restaurants around Ticarethane Sokak and İncili Çavuş Sokak off Divan Yolu. These are the neighbourhood's best and most lively, although they only really cater to tourists rather than locals and the touts out front can be a real turn-off.

For the best and most diverse dining in İstanbul, head to Beyoğlu, where you will find everything from canteen-style cheap eats on İstiklal Caddesi and cosy backstreet İskender restaurants (grills) to high-end dining with the city's jet set.

Be sure to take your fill from İstanbul's greatest culinary resource: the sea. From Ortaköy and up through the Bosphorus villages on the European shore, there are scores of seafood restaurants serving the catch of the day.

Rooftop dining

When the summer is at its most scorching, İstanbullus seek the balmy night-time relief of the city's rooftops. Starting from mid-May, restaurants all around İstanbul open up their rooftop terraces for alfresco dining with spectacular views. The best of the bunch are über trendy 360 (see page 56) and Nu Teras in Beyoğlu, and Vogue (see page 115) in Beşiktaş. For a more straightforward kebab with a view, try longstanding favourite Hamdi in Eminönü (see page 110).

Anchovies for sale in Kumkapı

Tempting baklava

WHAT TO EAT

Breakfast

A traditional Turkish breakfast consists of a hard-boiled egg with bread, olives, white cheese, tomatoes, cucumbers and honey. Washed down with small glasses of strong, sugary black tea, it can provide quite a springboard for your day. Otherwise, İstanbullus head to the bakery, where copious amounts of *börek* (made with filo pastry, and often filled with cheese), *poğaça* (bread rolls) and *simit* (an O-shaped roll topped with sesame seeds) are consumed in the morning and throughout the day too.

Ottoman cuisine

Simply by looking at the vast kitchens inside Topkapı Palace, you can tell that the culture of eating held a very important place in imperial life. The dishes consumed by the sultans are the stuff of legend; in the time of Süleyman the Magnificent, there were more than 150 recipes for preparing aubergine alone.

Most restaurants today serve hybrid versions of these dishes; however, there are a handful, such as Asitane next to the Kariye Museum (see page 82), that are devoted to reproducing the food from palace kitchens and imperial feasts. Dishes to look out for are *kavun dolma* (stuffed melon), *hünkar beğendi* (lamb with smoked aubergine puree), *mahmudiyye* (chicken stewed with apricots, almonds and grapes) and *zırba*

yahnisi (duck stewed in a clay casserole dish with a pastry crust).

Kebabs

Turkish kebabs are not as straightforward as they first appear. There is a range of different styles from various parts of the country. Most familiar to Westerners is the *döner* – meat piled up on a rotating spit that is then either rolled in flat durum bread or served in a sandwich. At a sit-down restaurant, you might prefer to try a *şiş kepab* (shish kebab), marinated chunks of chicken or lamb skewered and grilled, or a plate of *köfte*, grilled meatballs. *Adana* kebabs from the east of Turkey are good for those who like their meat spicy.

Not for the faint-hearted

Adventurous gourmands with hardy stomachs could try some of İstanbul's more unusual specialities. Ditch the kebab in favour of *kokoreç*, chopped lamb's intestines fried with pepper and onion, or try some *iskembe çorbası*, tripe soup. Also on the appetisers list are *beyin salatası* (lamb's brain salad) and *çiğ köfte* (raw lamb and pounded wheat meatballs). Finish off with *tavuk göğsü* (a milky pudding made from shredded chicken breast) for dessert.

Seafood

As İstanbul is a seaside city with a strong Greek influence, fish restaurants are among the most popular with locals. Often eaten in a *meyhane* (see box), fish

Simits make filling snacks

tends to be prepared very simply: fried or grilled *levrek* (sea bass), *palamut* (bonito) and *çupra* (bream) are served with a side salad and best enjoyed with a glass of *rakı*, an aniseed-based alcoholic beverage similar to Greek ouzo. Deep-fried *kalamar* (squid) are a first-course favourite, as are *hamsi* (fried anchovies), *midye tava* (deep fried mussels) and their stuffed counterparts, *midye dolması*, which contain rice, pine nuts, raisins and cinnamon. For fish on the go, head for one of the stands by the water at Eminönü.

Vegetarian options

With grilled meat and fish reigning supreme, İstanbul is hardly a vegetarian's paradise. There are, however, options for non-carnivores. They are most abundant among *meze* menus, which regularly feature *çacık* (strained yoghurt with garlic and cucumber), *patlıcan salatası* (aubergine salad), *fasulye* (fava beans) and a variety of *dolma* (vine leaves stuffed with fragrant rice); these last could include meat, so be sure to check first.

Most Turkish restaurants will also offer *mercemek*, a delicious lentil soup, although caution should be exercised here too, as traces of meat among the pulses are not unusual. *Zeytinyağlı*, a cold appetiser dish of vegetables, such as green beans or artichoke cooked in olive oil, is another very common vegetarian option.

Menemen (sloppy scrambled egg with tomatoes, peppers and white cheese) is a popular breakfast or lunch dish, mopped up with bread.

Desserts

Turkey makes no secret of its national sweet tooth, with ubiquitous pudding shops as well as cafés and bakeries exclusively devoted to the production of desserts.

Don't leave without sampling *baklava* (a sticky, layered filo-pastry dessert with ground pistachios or walnuts and honey) or its cousin *kadayif*, which is similar in taste, but made with shredded dough. Milk-based *sütlaç* (rice pudding) and *keşkül* (almond pudding) are commonly dished up as desserts, as are cooked fruits served chilled, like *incir* (fig), *ayva* (quince) and *armut* (pear). Be sure to

Meyhanes

When there's a call for celebration or just a lively night out, İstanbullus go 'meyhane'ye' (to the *meyhane*), a much-loved local style of restaurant based loosely on the Greek taverna. Most of the city's best *meyhanes* are located around Asmalı Mescit Caddesi and Nevizade Sokak (see page 59) in Beyoğlu; they are especially buzzing at weekends, when tables and chairs spill out onto the street and live music is played for the *rakı*-swilling clientele. It's customary to order a set menu at a *meyhane*, which includes a selection of *meze* followed by the fish of your choice with salad and a fresh-fruit dessert. Be sure to go with an appetite.

Mixing a drink in İstanbul Modern's café

sample some Turkish Delight at the Egyptian Bazaar; known locally as *lokum*, this world-famous regional treat is made from water, sugar, starch and rosewater.

Herbs and spices

Piles of spices at street markets look gorgeous and make perfect souvenirs as they're lightweight and travel well. Try to avoid buying ground spices: it is much better to buy the seeds and grind them yourself back home. *Pul biber* consists of coarse, dried pepper flakes and are used either as a cooking ingredient or just to sprinkle on white cheese and salads. They come in various degrees of heat, from sweet to fiery and chilli-like. *Aci biber* is similar, and sold as a paste which you stir into stews and soups to give them a kick.

The deep purple flakes of sumac are made from the berries of a sumac bush,

and have a slightly sour flavour. They can be rubbed into meat or fish before grilling, sprinkled onto rice or over a salad in place of lemon juice. Dried sage leaves make the refreshing drink *adachai*.

WHAT TO DRINK

Although Turkey is known for its tar-like thick black coffee *(kahve)*, its national drink is in fact tea *(çay)*, served in small tulip-shaped glasses with plenty of sugar and no milk. It's anyone's guess how much of the brew is consumed in the city on a daily basis, but the number of *çaycıs* (tea vendors) that can be seen around the streets with trays of tea attest to the nation's addiction.

On a more nutritious note, *taze portakal suyu* (fresh orange juice) is available from numerous street vendors, as are local specialities like *ayran*, a yoghurt drink, *sahlep*, a hot winter staple made from ground orchid root, and *boza*, a fermented wheat drink that was popular with the Ottoman janissaries (see page 77).

Outdoor dining on Sofyalı Sokak in Beyoğlu

Food and Drink Prices

Throughout this book, the price guide for a two-course dinner for one with a glass of wine (where available) is:

$$$$ = over 70YTL
$$$ = 40–70YTL
$$ = 20–40YTL
$ = under 20YTL

Embroidered kaftans

SHOPPING

With a bazaar culture that spans centuries, the Turks certainly love to shop. From the Grand Bazaar itself to the chic boutiques of Nişantaşı to hyper–modern malls like Kanyon, İstanbul has something to sell you on every corner.

BAZAARS

The Grand Bazaar should be any dedicated shopper's first port of call in İstanbul. Crammed in among chaotic covered streets and alleys, its thousands of stalls hold all manner of items, such as carpets and kilims (see box), leather, suede and denim clothes and accessories, ceramic tiles, bowls and vases, hand-beaten copper and brass lamps, coffee-grinders and samovars, gold and silver jewellery (beware imitations) and much more.

A paradise for some, the crowds and hawkers, and indeed the sheer size of the bazaar, can render the experience quite nightmarish for others. As a result, some shoppers prefer the smaller Egyptian (or Spice) Bazaar in Eminönü. As well as offering the typical souvenirs found in its larger cousin, the Egyptian Bazaar sells vast quantities of herbs and spices, as well as delicious candies and mixed nuts. It's also a good place to buy a *nargile* (water pipe) and accompanying fruit-flavoured molasses (see page 60). Note that the hillside area between these two landmarks is itself a massive warren of open street-markets, where locals barter fiercely for clothing, kitchenware and hardware.

Shoppers in the Egyptian Bazaar

MALLS

Although thousands of Turks visit the Grand Bazaar on a daily basis, İstanbul's 21st-century shoppers prefer the modern surroundings of the city's newly built malls. One to visit, not just for its stores but for its unusual appearance, is Kanyon (Büyükdere Caddesi 185; www.kanyon.com.tr) at the Levent Metro stop to the north of Taksim. An architectural curiosity, shaped like a steel-and-glass canyon, this indoor-outdoor mall houses

Fabric stall in the Grand Bazaar

Turkish designer brands as well as İstanbul's Harvey Nichols. On the same Metro line, between Levent and Taksim, at the Şişli stop, is sparkling Cevahir (Büyükdere Caddesi 22; www.istanbulcevahir.com), one of the largest malls in Europe. Its air-conditioned interior is perfect for escaping extreme weather conditions.

BOUTIQUES AND HIGH-END FASHION

Beyoğlu's main street, İstiklal Caddesi, is the place to go for high-street fashions, but for upmarket boutiques and big-name labels, head to the chic neighbourhood of Nişantaşı, 10 minutes by dolmuş from Taksim Square or Beşiktaş. Here, Armani, Gucci and Prada sit side by side with some of Turkey's most exclusive designers like Gönül Pasköy and Atıl Kutoğlu.

Nişantaşı is home to one of Turkey's ritziest fashion department stores, Beymen (Abdi İpekçi Caddesi 23/1; www.beymen.com.tr; daily). A style institution, Beymen has launched many names in Turkish high-end design, as well as showcasing international giants like Chanel and Dior. Leave time for lunch at the shop's fantastic brasserie.

ANTIQUES

In addition to the antiques in the Old Bazaar (İç Bedesten), the first place to look is the neighbourhood of Çukurcuma. A short walk from İstiklal Caddesi, tiny stores dotting Turnacıbaşı Sokak and Faik Paşa Yokuşu house a repository of artefacts from the late-Ottoman period and the early days of the Republic. Reputable antiques dealers should provide you with an invoice *(fatura)* for your purchase and organise an export permit. Although not as picturesque, the 200 stores spread across the six floors of Horhor Bit Pazarı (Horhor Caddesi, Aksaray; Mon–Sat) are full of finds for bargain hunters.

Carpets and rugs

İstanbul is one of the best places in the world to purchase a carpet, rug or kilim (a woven rather than knotted rug). The carpet merchants at the Grand Bazaar stock everything from fine silk Persian rugs to traditional, home-woven Anatolian kilims and prayer rugs. It's worth doing a bit of research before shelling out; in fact, lengthy price negotiations with the vendor can be part of the fun. Carpet prices reflect the age, rarity, quality of materials and dyes, tightness of weave and amount of work put in. The number of knots in a square centimetre ranges from 20–30 for a coarse wool carpet to 100–200 in a silk carpet. Natural dyes cost more than synthetic ones.

Inside the Grand Bazaar, you could try Şişko Osman in the relatively peaceful Zincirli Han (see page 47); outside, check out Noah's Ark on Ticarethane Sokak (off Divan Yolu; www.noahsark rugs.com).

Ghetto nightclub

ENTERTAINMENT

The days when a belly–dancing show was the best option for a Saturday night are long gone. Bars, clubs and late–night cafés have flourished in Beyoğlu, making the city's nightlife a match for the most lively of European capitals.

WHERE TO GO

The main area for a night on the Turkish tiles is Beyoğlu and İstiklal Caddesi, where the backstreets reverberate with the sounds of bass-heavy techno, live acoustic guitar or jazz trumpets.

Begin the night with a drink in any one of the small local bars on Bekar Sokak and Kurabiye Sokak. Further down İstiklal Caddesi, near the Galatasaray Lycée, Balo Sokak is also packed with bars and music venues, while nearby Nevizade Sokak teems with revellers eating and drinking at the *meyhanes* and outdoor bars (see page 59).

At the lower end of İstiklal Caddesi is attractive but more subdued Tünel, for those who prefer bohemian chatter over a bottle of wine.

In summer, you can party hard in the outdoor super-clubs on the Bosphorus shore near Ortaköy (see page 66), or chill out in the smaller, cosier bars at the centre of the village.

Except for the raucous travellers' bars on Akbıyık Sokak in Sultanahmet, the Old City is relatively inactive at night; if you prefer a quiet supper and early bed, that's the place for you.

BARS AND PUBS

Turkey might be an Islamic country, but the centre of İstanbul is anything but dry. Recent years have seen a proliferation in the number of watering holes in the city, from English- and Irish-style pubs (The North Shield and the James Joyce) to local holes in the wall (Küçük Cambaz) where the beers come cheap enough to stay all night. Wine-lovers should check out Pano, a century-old wine taverna, which also serves food alongside its own-label wines.

For less grunge and more bling, head to the legendary 360 (see page 56), Leb-i Derya or the Zoë Lounge and Club for cocktails with views to die for.

NIGHTCLUBS

Some İstanbullus take their clubbing very seriously; those that do make a beeline for the house, electronica and techno at established favourite Indigo. Relative newcomer The Hall is increasingly popular too. Both clubs are known for their colourful line-up of local and international DJs who lead the weekend party into the small hours.

Klub Karaoke

The Bosphorus clubs such as Reina and Angelique are a must during the summer months, as is the downtown rooftop Nu Teras, which switches from a restaurant into a nightclub late at weekends. For something a little more chilled, there's Ghetto, a bakery converted into a stage for world music.

LIVE MUSIC

İstanbul is flourishing with venues for live music of all varieties. The annual classical and jazz festivals organised by the İstanbul Foundation for Culture and Arts take place in June and July respectively, and there's a blues festival in November. Previously held at the Ataturk Kultur Merkezi (cultural centre) in Taksim Square, ballet, opera and recitals now take place in Kadikoy, on the Asian side (Bahariye Cadessi 29, Kadikoy; www.kadikoy.bel.tr). Jazz enthusiasts will find like minds at the Nardis Jazz Club in Galata.

One of the best venues for contemporary local music, from fiery ethnic sounds to hip hop, is Babylon in Tünel, while nearby Badehane (see page 55) is the venue for boisterous Wednesday nights powered by local gypsy-music icon Selim Sesler. In summer, keep an eye on the listings for weekend music festivals, which often feature big international stars.

Türkü is a popular style of music that gives a contemporary flavour to traditional songs. Lively bars offering türkü music can be found on either side of the Taksim end of İstiklal Caddesi.

GAY SCENE

İstanbul is one of the few places in the country where there is an active gay scene, with a set of clubs and bars known for their same-sex preferences. The gay scene is subject to fluctuation, but there are a few venues that have stood the test of time, like Tek Yön, or try the upmarket Penthouse Club in Taksim. The best place to start is at the laid-back Sugar & Spice in Beyoğlu, where you can find information about events and special club nights across the city. Nightlife for lesbians is much thinner on the ground. Bigudi, a café, bar and club, is a current favourite.

Live music at Nardis Jazz Club

Çemberlitaş Hamam

TURKISH BATHS

Although not as prevalent as they once were, Turkish baths are still an essential experience when visiting İstanbul. There are several historic hamams where bathers are scrubbed on steaming marble slabs from dawn 'til dusk.

The Turks inherited their bath culture by way of Roman and Byzantine *thermae* and Arab *hamams*. Until the advent of home plumbing and private bathrooms, a visit to the baths had been a communal activity that could last for hours, as entire families would spend the day bathing, talking, eating and even dancing.

The most notable *hamams* in İstanbul are those built by Ottoman architect Sinan (see page 76); the Haseki Hurram, Çemberlitaş and Süleymaniye *hamams* are all great examples of a bath house built around a circular *sıcaklık*, where a domed roof pierced by tiny glass windows allows light to fall in shafts through the steam. At the centre of the *sıcaklık* is a large heated marble slab upon which bathers relax and perspire prior to and after bathing.

VISITING A HAMAM

First-time visitors to a *hamam* are often a little apprehensive as to what will be involved. However, İstanbul's two most prominent bathhouses, Çemberlitaş and Çağaloğlu, cater extremely well to tourists, with price lists and instructions clearly posted in several languages. Note that most hamams are gender segregated.

You can just pay the basic fee to enter the *hamam* if you would prefer to wash yourself. Otherwise there are a number of different price options, depending on the kind of scrub you go for. Oil massages are administered in a separate room.

Getting changed

Upon entering the *hamam*, you will be shown to a changing room (gender-segregated), where you can undress and leave your belongings in a locker. Here you will be handed a pair of wooden clogs and a *pestemal* (towel) to wrap around yourself, before being invited to lie down upon the hot marble slab in the *sıcaklık* to sweat your tensions away.

In segregated *hamams*, women will usually strip down entirely and cover themselves in a *pestemal* before and after washing, although some women prefer to wear underwear. Men usually keep their *pestemals* wrapped tightly around the waist for the duration. If in doubt, ask an attendant what they would recommend

Lavender soap on sale   *Pestemals*

A HAMAM DICTIONARY

During your visit, you might encounter the following:

Kese. A washcloth woven from mohair, a *kese* is used in the hot room to exfoliate the skin. Once a bather has spent some time lying on the hot marble in the steam of the *sıcaklık*, softened skin is vigorously rubbed with a *kese*.

Nalin. These traditional *hamam* clogs are essentially a piece of wood raised off the floor by two wooden blocks. Although tricky to walk in, they lift your feet up from the *hamam* floor and prevent slipping.

Pestemal. Usually made from cotton, but also available in silk, a *pestemal* is a piece of white fabric used to wrap around the body. These towels are woven very thin, so that they dry quickly after being soaked in the hot room.

Sisal. Similar to a *kese*, this washcloth is made from the rough fibres of an agave plant. It is used for deep exfoliation and the stimulation of blood circulation in the body.

İSTANBUL'S HAMAMS

Çağaloğlu Hamam

Prof. Kazım Ismail Gürkan Caddesi 34, Çağaloğlu; tel: 0212 522 2424; www.cagalogluhamami.com.tr; daily 8am–10pm for men, 8am–8pm for women; entry: $25, soap scrub and massage: $65

The most famous of all the *hamams* not just for its beauty but for its past rollcall of illustrious customers including Florence Nightingale and Rudolf Nureyev. This 18th-century building is a popular haunt for tourists in Sultanahmet.

Çemberlitaş Hamam

Vezirhan Caddesi 8, Çemberlitaş; tel: 0212 522 7974; www.cemberlitashamami.com.tr; daily 6am–midnight; entry: $26, traditional soap scrub and massage: $38, oil massage: $65

Probably the most popular *hamam* with tourists, this historic building near the Grand Bazaar was built in 1584 by Sinan, and is clean and well managed.

Galatasaray Hamam

Turnaçıbaşı Sokak 24, Galatasaray; tel: 0212 252 4242 (men), 0212 249 4342 (women); www.galatasarayhamami.com; daily 7am–10pm for men, 8am–9pm for women; entry: $32, soap scrub and massage: $58

The central location of this *hamam*, in a backstreet off İstiklal Caddesi, is its strongest point. The separate women's section is small.

Süleymaniye Hamam

Mimar Sinan Caddesi 20, Süleymaniye; tel: 0212 519 5569; www.suleymaniyehamami.com; daily 10am–midnight; entry: $24, soap scrub and massage: $46

A quieter, more secluded option, this is one of the few *hamams* that is not segregated and only has male washing attendants. Not surprisingly it is usually filled with tourists.

Painting of the Harem by Jean–Baptiste Vanmour (c.1720–37)

HISTORY: KEY DATES

Once a humble Greek fishing village, then the seat of two empires, now a modern industrial metropolis, Istanbul has been shaped by military conquests, strident leaders, religious creeds, bloody riots and destructive earthquakes.

BEGINNINGS OF BYZANTIUM

*c.*660BC	Megarian leader Byzas establishes Byzantium at the confluence of the Golden Horn, the Bosphorus and the Sea of Marmara.
512	Persian domination of the city begins. Darius builds a bridge of boats in an unsuccessful bid to conquer Eastern Europe.
478	Greek rule returns to Byzantium under Pausanias of Sparta.
279	Byzantium repulses invasion by the Celts, but agrees to pay tribute.
179	Rhodes, Pergamum and Bithynia join forces to conquer city. Byzantium becomes part of the Roman Empire.
195AD	Roman Emperor Septimius Severus sacks Byzantium for siding with his rivals in a civil war.

BYZANTINE CONSTANTINOPLE

330	Roman Emperor Constantine builds his new capital in the city and names it Constantinople, beginning the Byzantine era.
395	Death of Theodosius I; final division of Roman Empire.
413–47	Theodosius II builds city walls.
532–7	Construction of Hagia Sophia (Aya Sofya).
674–8	First Arab siege of Constantinople.
1071	Seljuk Turks defeat Byzantines at Malazgirt and sweep into Anatolia, triggering the Crusades.
1204	Christian crusaders sack Constantinople and establish a Latin kingdom in the city.
1261	Byzantine rule of Constantinople restored.
1326	The Osmanli Turks capture Bursa; the Ottoman Empire is born.

The Orient Express

OTTOMAN CAPITAL

1453	Sultan Mehmet II conquers Constantinople and names it İstanbul.
C.16th	Ottoman rule reaches zenith under Süleyman the Magnificent. Empire extends from the gates of Vienna to North Africa.
C.17th	Ottoman Empire begins a slow 300-year decline as a result of military defeats, changes in trade routes and failure to keep up with technological advances in western Europe.
1914–18	Ottoman Empire sides with Germany and Austria-Hungary during World War I.
1919–22	İstanbul occupied by the Allied forces. The Turks, under Mustafa Kemal, engage in War of Independence. The sultanate is abolished.

REPUBLICAN ERA

1923	Independent Republic of Turkey is established, with a new capital in Ankara. Mustafa Kemal, later known as Atatürk, becomes president.
1920s–30s	Atatürk carries out sweeping reforms.
1938	Atatürk dies in İstanbul.
1952	Turkey joins NATO.
1973	Bosphorus Bridge completed.

MODERN İSTANBUL

1995	Customs Union agreement signed with EU.
1998	Kurdish separatists (the PKK) begin an armed insurrection in southeastern Turkey; İstanbul suffers intermittent bomb attacks.
1999	17 August: İstanbul earthquake; thousands perish.
2003	Iraq War. Al Qa'eda targets İstanbul with bombs at two synagogues, the British Consulate and HSBC Bank.
2005	Start of formal talks on making Turkey a member of the EU.
2010	İstanbul is European Capital of Culture.
2013	Proposed development plans for Gezi Park in Taksim Square develop into riots when a group occupying the park are attacked by police.

BEST ROUTES

Basilica Cistern

SULTANAHMET: AROUND HAGIA SOPHIA

Descend into the magical depths of the Underground Cistern, marvel at the stunning architecture of Hagia Sophia, then explore the streets of historic Sultanahmet, before winding down with a relaxing hamam.

DISTANCE: 2.5km (1.5 miles)
TIME: A leisurely day
START: The Milion
END: Çemberlitaş Hamam
POINTS TO NOTE: This is the first of two tours of Sultanahmet (see also route 2). The main sights could be packed into one full day, but are best spread out over two. Note that Hagia Sophia is closed on Mondays.

Jutting out into the water, where the Bosphorus and the Golden Horn meet the Sea of Marmara (Marmara Denizi), is the historic district of Sultanahmet. This was the site of the original Byzantium, founded in the 7th century BC, and later the site of the civic centre of Constantinople, capital of the Byzantine Empire. Here, too, the conquering Ottoman sultanate established its seat of power from the 15th century onward.

Home to some of İstanbul's most important monuments, and the first port of call for visitors to the city, the beautifully restored neighbourhood is very

much geared towards tourism, so be prepared for the tiresome attention of touts.

LAYOUT

At the centre of the historic district is Sultanahmet Park, bordered to the south by the Blue Mosque and to the north by the magnificent Hagia Sophia. To the east of the park are Sultanahmet's backstreets, known as Cankurtaran, home to dozens of hotels and guesthouses set within old Ottoman houses, while the district's main street, Divan Yolu, branches off to the west, towards the Çemberlitaş Hamam and the Grand Bazaar.

THE MILION

Begin just to the west of Hagia Sophia in the small park between Yerebatan Caddesi and Divan Yolu. It is perhaps a fitting place to begin these tours of İstanbul, as this was the location of the **Milion ❶**, a triumphal archway from the time of Emperor Constantine in the 4th century, which was the marker

Four Seasons Hotel Istanbul   *Byzantine mosaic, Hagia Sophia*

from which all distances in the Eastern Roman Empire were measured. From here stretched the main thoroughfare of Constantinople (now Divan Yolu) to the city gates and the empire beyond. A small section of a stone pillar is all that remains today.

BASILICA CISTERN

Just behind on Yerebatan Caddesi, look for the small rectangular building, at no. 13, which marks the entrance to the **Basilica Cistern ❷** (Yerebatan Sarnıcı; tel: 0212 522 1259; www.yerebatan. com; daily 9am–6.30pm; charge). This bewitching, elegantly lit construction is part of the city's ancient system of underground reservoirs, which was fed by water from the Belgrade Forest to the north of the city. The cistern measures 140m (460ft) by 70m (230ft); its vaulted brick roof is supported by a forest of columns topped by Corinthian capitals, 336 in all, set in 12 rows of 28.

Built under Justinian in 532AD, it was in use during the Byzantine era, but forgotten thereafter until 1545, when a Frenchman discovered that residents drew water from wells in their homes. The cistern was brought back into use as the water supply for Topkapı, and eventually restored and opened to visitors in 1987. As you make your way along the walkways between the columns, you can marvel at the fact that

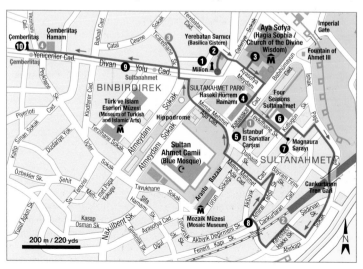

Arabic medallion beneath Hagia Sophia's dome

this remarkable feat of engineering still stands, 1,500 years after it was built.

HAGIA SOPHIA

Cross the road and walk to the majestic coral-pink edifice that is the definitive emblem of old İstanbul and the most awe-inspiring of the city's Byzantine remains. **Hagia Sophia** ❸ (Aya Sofya in Turkish, the Church of the Divine Wisdom in English; Tue–Sun mid-Apr–Oct 9am–7pm, Nov–mid-Apr 9am–5pm, last entry 1 hour before closing; charge) was for almost 1,000 years the greatest church in Christendom.

History
It is thought that Emperor Constantine built a Christian basilica here in AD325

on the site of a pagan temple. It was destroyed by fire in 404 and rebuilt by Theodosius II, then burnt down again in 532. The building you see today was commissioned by Justinian and completed in 537, although many repairs, additions and alterations have been made over the centuries.

The finest materials were used in its construction – white marble from the islands of the Marmara, verd antique from Thessaly, yellow marble from Africa, gold and silver from Ephesus, and ancient red porphyry columns that possibly came from Egypt. The interior was covered with golden mosaics, lit by countless flickering candelabras.

The last Christian service ever to be held in what was then the Hagia Sophia took place on 28 May 1453, the day before Constantinople fell to the Turks. Mehmet the Conqueror immediately converted the building to an imperial mosque, and built a brick minaret at the southeast corner. The architect Sinan (see page 76) strengthened the buttresses and added the other three minarets during the 16th century, and Hagia Sophia served as a mosque until 1935, when Atatürk decreed that it should become a museum.

Inside the museum
The entrance path leads past the ticket desk towards the main portal, which is surrounded by architectural fragments from the 5th-century church built by Theodosius. The scale of the interior is

Not Constantinople

İstanbul has undergone several name changes over the ages, as celebrated in the 1950s song *İstanbul (Not Constantinople)*. The Greek colony, founded on the site of what is today Sultanahmet in the 7th century BC, came to be known as Byzantion (Latinised as Byzantium) after its founder, King Byzas. When Constantine decided to make the city the new capital of the Eastern Roman Empire in 330AD, it became Constantinople, 'Constantine's City'. After the Ottoman conquest in 1453 the Turks called their capital İstanbul, 'to the city'.

Hagia Sophia's exterior view

overwhelming: the dome is around 31m (102ft) in diameter, and floats 55m (180ft) above the floor. The sensation of space is created by the absence of supporting walls beneath the dome. It was the achievement of architects Isidorus and Anthemius to transfer the weight of the dome to the pillars using semi-domes and arches to create the illusion of an unsupported dome.

To the left of the entrance is the "sweating column", where Justinian was said to have cured a migraine by resting his head against the stone, leading to the belief that, when rubbed, each of the church's pillars could cure a specific disease.

The original decoration has long since disappeared. Eight huge medallions, bearing the Arabic names of Allah, Mohammed, two of his grandsons and the first four caliphs, and a quotation from the Qur'an in the crown of the dome, are remnants of Hagia Sophia's 500-plus years as an imperial mosque, as are the elaborate *mihrab* (the niche in the wall pointing to Mecca) and *mimber* (pulpit) in the apse. However, a handful of Christian mosaics survive, mostly on the second floor (see box).

As you leave by the door on the ground floor at the southern end of the narthex, turn around and look up to see a 10th-century mosaic of emperors Constantine and Justinian offering symbols of Constantinople and the Hagia Sophia to the Virgin Mary and Child.

CANKURTARAN

Across from Hagia Sophia, at the eastern edge of Sultanahmet Park, are the **Baths of Roxelana** ❹ (Haseki Hürrem Hamamı; tel: 0212 517 3535; www.ayasofyahamami.com; daily 7am–midnight), built by Sinan in 1556 for the wife of Süleyman the Magnificent. The building languished over the years, until 2011 when it was restored to its original use as a Turkish bath house.

Take a right from here down the quaint Kabasakal Caddesi for a cup of tea in the garden of the handsome **Yeşil Ev Hotel**, see ❶, set inside an old Ottoman

Byzantine mosaics

In its days as a Byzantine cathedral, the walls of Hagia Sophia were covered with glittering mosaics, most of which were plastered over or damaged after the Ottoman conquest when the church was converted to a mosque. However, a few remain: above the apse, for example, is a depiction of the Virgin and the infant Jesus, with the Archangel Gabriel to the right. The best fragments can be seen up in the second-floor galleries: by the southern wall is the *Deesis*, an extraordinary 13th-century mosaic showing Christ flanked by the Virgin Mary and St John the Baptist. On the eastern wall are two images showing Byzantine emperors and empresses making offerings to Christ on his throne and to the Virgin and Child.

The Four Seasons is a former prison

mansion. Afterwards, head next door to the **Handicrafts Centre** ❺ (İstanbul El Sanatları Çarşısı; tel: 0212 517 6785; daily 9am–6.30pm) for a quiet, unhassled look around some small shops that sell calligraphy, embroidery, miniatures and ceramics.

Former prison
Retrace your steps to where Tevkifhane Sokak branches off to the right, and set off down this street past the **Four Seasons Sultanahmet** ❻ (see page 101). The large yellow hotel building was once a prison, and it is worth popping in to see the original prison doors and columns etched with inmates' graffiti. The legendary lock-up featured in the film *Midnight Express* (1978).

Magnaura Palace
At the bottom of this street you will see a shop called **Başdoğan Carpets**. Pass through to the courtyard at the back of the shop to discover the little-known underground remains of what used to be the Byzantine **Magnaura Palace** ❼ (Magnaura Sarayı), discovered by the shop's owner quite by chance. These interconnecting rooms were part of Constantine's Great Palace (see page 36), which covered an area equivalent to 16 soccer fields.

Tranquil backstreets
Continue from here down towards the edge of Sultanahmet, taking İshak Paşa Caddesi all the way to Cankurtaran Train

Station. Then head along Ahırkapı Sokak, which runs parallel to a stretch of remains of the old city walls on the edge of the Sea of Marmara. A good lunch option in this quieter, more residential area is **Giritli**, see ❷, a bright blue wooden house on the corner of Keresteci Hakkı and Şadırvan Sokak, which has a pretty summer garden.

This lower section of Sultanahmet around Cankurtaran is much quieter and reminiscent of the days prior to the onslaught of tourism. Continue along Keresteci Hakkı Sokak and turn right, passing back under the railway line. From here, turn right onto **Amiral Tafdil Sokak** ❽, where you will pass dozens of small boutique hotels set in the wooden Ottoman houses that line the street. A left on Bayram Fırını Sokak will lead you to the busy youth hostels and tourist cafés of Akbıyık Caddesi. Across the road here is a restored section of **Magnaura Palace's façade**.

DIVAN YOLU

Head back uphill to Sultanahmet Park, and cross over the top end of the Hippodrome (see page 35) to **Divan Yolu** ❾, the road that was (and still is) the main route leading to the city gates in Byzantine and Ottoman times. Just to the right as you walk along the street is **Ticarethane Sokak**, home to some of the area's better restaurants, including **Adonin**, see ❸.

Doorway in Cankurtaran   _Baths of Roxelana_

Constantine's Column

Some 500m/yds up Divan Yolu stands **Constantine's Column** ⑩ (Çemberli-taş), a stone pillar that rises to the right of the road. It was erected by Constantine in AD330 to mark the city's new status as capital of the Eastern Roman Empire, with parts of the cross and nails with which Christ was crucified reputedly sealed in the column's base. Also known as the Burnt Column, it was charred and cracked by a great fire that ravaged the district in 1770.

Çemberlitaş Hamam

Next door, at no. 8, is the **Çemberlitaş Hamam** (see page 23). Built by Sinan in 1584, the domed edifice is obscured by adjacent shops, and the doorway is easy to miss. Restored and fully functioning, this tourist-friendly hamam is one of the best and cleanest in the city, and is the perfect way to unwind after a day spent pounding the pavements of Old Stamboul. Further down Divan Yolu is **Cennet**, see ④, a quirky _gözleme_ (Turkish pancake) joint.

Food and Drink

① YEŞIL EV

Kabasakal Caddesi 5; tel: 0212 517 6785; www.istanbulyesilev.com; daily B, L, AT and D; $$

The outdoor garden of this beautifully restored Ottomanmansion-turned-hotel ('the Green House') is a great place to relax and grab a coffee mid-sightseeing. If you decide to eat here, you might want to try the _sarma_, minced meat and rice wrapped in vine leaves, or _güveç_, a stew baked in a clay pot.

② GIRITLI

Keresteci Hakkı Sokak; tel: 0212 458 2270; www.giritlirestoran.com; daily noon–midnight; $$$

An unpretentious little establishment set in quiet Cankurtaran, Giritli serves Greek- and Armenian-influenced _meze_ as well as fresh fish.

③ ADONIN

Ticarethane Sokak 27/31; tel: 0212 514 0029; www.adonincafe.com; daily 8am–midnight; $$$

Just off Divan Yolu, this attractive joint is pretty in the summer with a leafy outdoor seating, and cosy in the winter with a fireplace and good selection of magazines. The food is Ottoman-Anatolian and the service convivial.

④ CENNET

Divan Yolu Cd 31; tel: 0212 518 8111; daily 9am–10pm; $

This _gözleme_ (savoury pancake) café is somewhat on the tacky side – especially if you come for dinner, when you might be coerced into wearing panto-style Ottoman headgear. However, the meat, cheese and potato _gözleme_ are great value, and it is fascinating to watch the traditionally attired women make them in front of you.

The Blue Mosque

SULTANAHMET: AROUND THE BLUE MOSQUE

Continue your historical exploration of Sultanahmet by visiting the Blue Mosque and the site of the ancient Hippodrome. Pause for some shopping at the Arasta Bazaar, then resume at the Museum of Turkish and Islamic Arts.

DISTANCE: 2km (1.25 miles)
TIME: A half day
START: Tomb of Sultan Ahmet I
END: Museum of Turkish and Islamic Arts
POINTS TO NOTE: The Blue Mosque opens at sunrise; get there early to beat the crowds. Women should wear a headscarf.

Sultan Ahmet

Sultan Ahmet I, commissioner of the Blue Mosque, ascended the throne at the age of 12 and reigned from 1603 to 1617, dying at just 27. He was a deeply religious man with a love of writing poetry, which he penned under the name of Bahti. His wife, Köşem Sultan, was one of the most powerful women in the Ottoman state; she ruled the Harem and (historians suggest) the empire for nearly 50 years through her husband, two sons and grandson Mehmet IV.

The Sultanahmet that is seen today owes its immediate appearance to the Ottomans, although its layout is altogether more ancient, having been built upon the ruins of the Hippodrome and Great Palace of Constantine. The domes of the magnificent Blue Mosque continue to dominate the skyline, while the majestic façade of Ibrahim Paşa's former palace looks across the former heart of the Byzantine city.

TOMB OF SULTAN AHMET

Begin at the **Tomb of Sultan Ahmet I ❶** (Sultan Ahmet Türbesi; Tue–Sun 9.30am–4.30pm; free), the ruler after whom the district is named (see box). The small domed building just to the north of the Blue Mosque and to the east of the Hippodrome on Sultanahmet Square also housed his wife, three sons and other relatives.

HIPPODROME

Walk a few steps to the elongated plaza, studded with column-like struc-

The Egyptian Obelisk   *Door to the Tomb of Sultan Ahmet I*

tures, which is known as the **Hippodrome ❷** (At Meydanı). Inspired by the Circus Maximus in Rome, it was built in AD203 as a stadium for chariot racing and other public events. Later it was enlarged by Constantine the Great to hold an audience of 100,000, becoming the civic centre of the Byzantine capital. In AD532, 30,000 rioting citizens were killed here during the Nika revolt.

The top (northern) end of the *spina*, or central axis, is marked by an ornate domed ablutions **fountain**, given to the city by Germany's Kaiser Wilhelm II to commemorate his visit in 1900. At the opposite end rise three remnants of the original Hippodrome. The **Egyptian Obelisk** (also known as the Obelisk of Theodosius/Theodosius Dikiltaşı) dates back to the 16th century BC and was brought to the city from Egypt by Theodosius in AD390. The **Serpentine Column** (Yılanlı Sütun), the oldest Greek monument in the city, commemorates the Greek victory over the Persians at Plataea in 479BC (it was brought here from Delphi by Constantine the Great). The **Column of Porphyrogenitus** (Örme Dikiltaşı) dates from the 10th century AD.

Only one section of the Hippodrome's **original wall ❸** can still be seen today, on the far southern side of the square.

BLUE MOSQUE

From the Hippodrome, make your way into the courtyard of the **Blue Mosque ❹**, also known as the Sultan Ahmet Camii after its patron, Ahmet I, who had the edifice constructed in 1616. As you pass through the portal, let your eyes be swept up by the crescendo of domes that top the building.

One of the most magnificent shrines in the Muslim world, its six minarets were controversial at the time of construction as they equalled

The Blue Mosque's interior

those of the El Haram Mosque surrounding the Kaaba in Mecca. The architect, Mehmet Ağa, was consequently sent to Mecca to add another minaret to the mosque, thereby preserving its seniority.

Inside the mosque

Follow the courtyard around to the right and look for the signs to the visitors' entrance. Once inside you will see how the mosque earned its familiar name: more than 20,000 turquoise İznik tiles glow gently in the light from the mosque's 260 windows, decorated with lilies, carnations, tulips and roses. Four massive columns support a dome 22m (70ft) in diameter and 43m (142ft) high at the crown – big, but not quite as big as Hagia Sophia, the design of which clearly influenced the architect.

The *mihrab* and *mimber* are of carved white marble, and the ebony window shutters are inlaid with ivory and mother-of-pearl. The painted blue arabesques in the domes and upper walls are restorations; to see the originals, look at the wall beneath the sultan's loge.

ARASTA BAZAAR

Take the northeastern exit out of the mosque into the gardens facing Hagia Sophia, and to your right you will see a short tunnel leading from the mosque complex down to the **Arasta Bazaar** ❺. Originally built as part of the Blue Mosque complex to attract rent reve-nue, this quiet street houses a number of carpet and collectors' shops, with a particularly interesting selection of antique and Central Asian fabrics.

If you fancy lunch now, leave the Arasta Bazaar via the northern entrance and cross Torun Sokak, bearing left to the picturesque whitewashed wooden house of **Rami**, see ❶.

MOSAIC MUSEUM

At the southern end of the bazaar is the **Mosaic Museum** ❻ (Mozaik Müzesi; tel: 0212 518 1205; Tue–Sun Nov–Mar 9am–5pm, Apr–Oct 9am–7pm, last entry 30 minutes before closing; charge), displaying the fascinating remains of the 6th-century mosaic floor of Constantine's Great Palace. It is well worth a visit to see the original Byzantine images contained in the mosaic fragments. The Great Palace was one of the grandest structures of Byzantine times and used to stretch all the way down to the Marmara Sea. The 4th-century palace contained 500 halls and 30 chapels as well as gold trees and mechanical birds. The mosaics are all that remain of it today.

KÜÇÜK HAGIA SOPHIA MOSQUE

After exploring the museum, head down Küçük Ayasofya Caddesi for 300m/yds to the beautiful **Küçük ('Little') Hagia Sophia Mosque** ❼ (Küçük Aya Sofya Camii), a former Byzantine church

Arasta Bazaar

turned mosque. Built by Justinian and Theodora in AD527 as the Church of Saints Sergius and Bacchus, it is a tiny replica of Hagia Sophia. Its mosaics are sadly no longer in place, but the dark-green and red marble columns and carved frieze are originals.

SOKULLU MEHMET PAŞA MOSQUE

Walk north and turn left on Kadırga Limanı Caddesi, which marks the start of **Kumkapı**, a former Byzantine fishing village a short walk from Sultanahmet. Take the second right to reach the **Sokullu Mehmet Paşa Mosque** ❽ (Sokullu Mehmet Paşa Camii). This mosque was built by Mimar Sinan in 1571 for Esma Sultan, the daughter of Selim the Sot and wife of Sokullu Mehmet Paşa, a highly regarded Bosnian-born grand vizier who was assassinated by a crazed Dervish in 1579. Inside are some of Turkey's finest 16th-century İznik tiles. Sokullu's mansion, just uphill, has been restored as the charming **Sokullu Paşa Hotel** (Mehmet Paşa Sokak 10).

MUSEUM OF TURKISH AND ISLAMIC ARTS

Exit the mosque down the steps of the main entrance of the courtyard, take a right and walk back up the hill to return to the Hippodrome. On the left-hand side is the **Museum of Turkish and Islamic Arts** ❾ (Türk ve İslam Eserleri Müzesi; tel: 0212 518 1805; closed for restoration until 2014), one of Turkey's best museums as well as one of İstanbul's finest Ottoman residential buildings. A Greek convert to Islam, Ibrahim Paşa was a close friend of the sultan and was married to Süleyman's sister Hatice, which explains the grandeur of his palace as well as its proximity to Topkapı. But Ibrahim Paşa's influence over the sultan roused the ire of other courtiers, including the sultan's favourite wife, Hürrem Sultan (Roxelana); he was strangled in 1536.

The museum contains over 40,000 items dating from the earliest period of Islam under the Omayyad caliphate (661–750), and specialises in religious artefacts and historic carpets. There's also a pleasant, traditional Ottoman-style coffeehouse on the ground floor.

Food and Drink

❶ RAMİ

Utangaç Sokak 6; tel: 0212 517 6593; www.ramirestaurant.com; daily noon–11pm; $$$

You can enjoy dinner with a view of the Blue Mosque in this romantic restaurant dedicated to the Turkish painter Rami Uluer. Home specialities include the *hunkar beğendi* (lamb with pureed aubergine) and *kağit kebabı* (a type of lamb kebab baked in wax paper).

Classical concert in Hagia Eirene

TOPKAPI PALACE

Explore the secret life of the Ottoman dynasty in their private quarters at Topkapı Palace, and look around the former throne rooms and pavilions from where the sultans used to govern the city and the entire empire.

DISTANCE: 2.5km (1.5 miles)
TIME: A half (or full) day
START/END: Fountain of Sultan Ahmet III
POINTS TO NOTE: Start early to avoid the crowds. There are separate tickets for the main palace and Harem, the latter sold from the ticket booth in front of the Harem entrance. The palace is closed on Tuesdays and the last tour of the Harem is at 4pm. Renovations of the palace are on-going so be prepared for sections to be closed.

For almost 400 years, **Topkapı Palace** (Topkapı Sarayı; tel: 0212 512 0480; www.topkapisarayi.gov.tr; Wed–Mon Apr–Sept 9am–7pm, Oct–Mar 9am–5pm; charge) was the residence of the Ottoman sultans, who ruled from this very spot a vast empire that stretched, at its zenith, from the gates of Vienna to the Indian Ocean, and from North Africa to the Crimean Peninsula.

Begun in 1462 by Mehmet the Conqueror, Topkapı Palace was extended by each succeeding sultan until it became a miniature city, which included mosques, libraries, stables, kitchens, schools, the imperial mint, treasuries, barracks, armouries and audience halls. At least 4,000 people lived within the complex, serving the imperial household.

Sultan Abdül Mecit moved into the newly built Dolmabahçe Palace in 1853 (see page 62), and by 1909 Topkapı was completely abandoned. In 1924 it was converted into a museum, and has been undergoing a continuous programme of restoration ever since.

FIRST COURT

This circular tour begins at the **Fountain of Ahmet III ❶** (Sultan Ahmet III Çeşmesi). The main entrance to the palace is through the **Imperial Gate** (Bab-ı-Hümayûn) opposite. The gate leads to the **First Court ❷** (Alay Meydanı), also known as the Court of the Janissaries (after the sultan's private infantry unit), where state processions began and ended.

Valide Sultan's Quarters   *Sultan's Bath in the Harem*

Hagia Eirene

To the left as you walk through the court is the city's earliest Byzantine church, **Hagia Eirene** ❸ (Aya Irini in Turkish, the Church of the Divine Peace in English). Constructed by Constantine the Great in the 4th century, it served as the patriarchal cathedral until the completion of Hagia Sophia (Aya Sofya), while the Ottomans used it as an arsenal. The only way to see the breathtakingly expansive domed ceiling is by attending one of the classical concerts of the İstanbul Music Festival in June.

SECOND COURT

Follow the path from Hagia Eirene towards the main entrance of the pal-

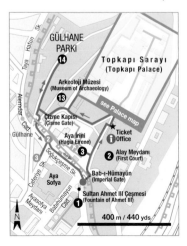

ace and buy your tickets from the booth on the right-hand side.

Pass through the **Gate of Salutations** (Bab-ı-Selam) to enter the **Second Court** ❹ (Divan Meydanı). The gate is considered the main entrance to the palace museum, and opens on to what was once a splendid garden full of peacocks and other exotic animals, where ceremonial processions and state banquets were held. To the far left is the entrance to the Harem, and on the immediate right are miniature models of Topkapı Palace as it was during the 16th century.

The Divan

Head to the left-hand side of the Second Court where you will find the **Divan** ❺, or Kubbe Altı (Hall Under the Dome). In this three-domed structure the Imperial Council met four times a week, reclining on cushioned benches *(divans)*. At the peak of empire, the Divan was one of the most powerful centres of government in Europe.

Next door to the Divan is the **Inner Treasury** (İç Hazine), a treat for weaponry enthusiasts. Formerly the office from where the janissaries were paid, it is now home to an exhibition of arms and armour, with 400 weapons from various Muslim empires. Dating from the 7th to the 20th century, helmets, swords and rifles sit alongside the highlight of the collection, the sword of Mehmet the Conqueror, with its gold-engraved inscriptions.

The Divan's tower

THIRD COURT

Walk to the **Third Court** ❻ (Enderûn Avlusu) through the **Gate of Felicity** (Baba-üs Saadet), once guarded by the white eunuchs, who were captured from Greek and Balkan lands and castrated before puberty, therefore considered trustworthy to guard the Harem. Ahead is the **Throne Room** (Arz Odası), where the sultan sat on ceremonial occasions and received viziers after sessions in the Divan. Just beyond is the **Library of Ahmet III**.

Many of the buildings in this court, particularly to the left as you enter, were once part of the Palace School;

one still functions as a library for Ottoman scholars.

Exhibition rooms

The first exhibition room on the left-hand side was once a dormitory, but now houses the **Sultans' Portraits Room** ❼ (Padişah Portreleri Sergi Salonu), which includes a copy of 15th-century Venetian painter Gentile Bellini's painting of Mehmet II.

One of the palace's most fascinating displays is in the adjacent **Pavilion of the Holy Mantle** (Hasoda Koğuşu), which contains some of the holiest relics of the Muslim world. They were mostly acquired by Selim the Grim in the early 16th century (see box).

Now cross to the opposite side, where the **Imperial Treasury** ❽ (Hazine Koğuşu) is home to the Ottoman collection of jewels and precious metals, including a diamond-encrusted suit of chain mail, the 18th-century emerald-studded Topkapı Dagger and the 84-carat Spoonmaker's Diamond. To the right is the **Hall of the Campaign Pages** (Seferli Koğuşu), which holds an exhibition of imperial costumes.

FOURTH COURT

Make your way through one of the two passageways on the northern side to the **Fourth Court** ❾ (Sofa-ı Hümâyûn). The palace's more informal quarters provided the sultans with breathtaking views of the Golden Horn from the terraces.

Sacred relics

Hairs from the Prophet Mohammed's beard, a holy tooth and a letter written by the Prophet are part of the collection of sacred relics kept in the Pavilion of the Holy Mantle. The Door of Repentance, taken from the Holy Kaaba in Mecca, dominates the first room, while the second contains Mohammed's footprint (set in clay) and a lock of his hair. An object of particular veneration for Muslims is the Felicitous Cloak (Hırka-i Saadet), woven by Mohammed's harem. It is kept in gold caskets along with the Sacred Standard (Sancakçerif). All of these sanctified artefacts are kept under the constant flow of the words of the Qur'an, recited by a Qari.

Tiles in the Harem

Imperial Hall in the Harem

The left-hand passageway leads along a corridor of pillars to a water fountain from where you can see **Revan Pavilion** ❿ (Revan Köşkü), built in 1635 to celebrate the Ottoman capture of the Armenian city of Erivan (Yerevan) from Persia; the **Baghdad Pavilion** (Bağdat Köşkü), a 17th-century reading room; and the gilded doorway and tiled exterior of the **Circumcision Room** (Sünnet Odası).

Cross over to the other side of the immense court to the Baroque **Mecidiye Pavilion** ⓫ (Mecidiye Köşkü), built by Abdül Mecit in the 19th century for the purpose of receiving guests. The lower floor of the pavilion hosts the **Konyalı Restaurant and Café**, see ❶, with a stunning patio overlooking the Sea of Marmara. It's an ideal setting for lunch.

THE HAREM

Retrace your steps to the middle of the Second Court and turn right. The **Harem** ⓬, which translates as 'forbidden', consists of more than 300 rooms, but only about 40 are open to the public, and these can be seen on a self-guided tour, which is worth taking especially with an audio guide (charge).

The Harem was a self-sustaining unit, which consisted of dormitories, private quarters, two small mosques, a school, a swimming pool and baths. Between 500 and 1,500 people lived within its walls, subject to strict discipline and a rigorous hierarchy. Life inside was not the den of debauchery

Bağdat Köşkü (Baghdad Pavilion)

Kiosk of Kara Mustafa Paşa

Sofa-ı Hümâyûn (Fourth Court) ❾

GÜLHANE PARKI

Mecidiye Köşkü (Mecidiye Pavilion) ⓫ ❶

Sofu Camii

Revan Köşkü (Revan Pavilion) ❿

Sünnet Odası (Circumcision Room)

Miniatures and Portrait Gallery

Hazine Koğuşu (Imperial Treasury) ❽

Hasoda Koğuşu (Pavilion of the Holy Mantle) ★

Enderûn Avlusu (Third Court) ❻

Padişah Portreleri Sergi Salonu (Sultans' Portraits Room) ❼

Library of Ahmet III

Seferli Koğuşu (Hall of the Campaign Pages) ★

Arz Odası (Throne Room)

Armoury

★ Bab-üs Saadet (Gate of Felicity)

İç Hazine (Inner Treasury) ★

Clock Room

Harem Entrance ⓬ ❺

Kubbe Altı (Divan)

Palace Kitchens

Council Chamber

H a r e m

Divan Meydanı (Second Court) ❹

Bab-ı Selam (Gate of Salutations)

100 m / 110 yds

Alay Meydanı (First Court)

Baldachin on Baghdad Pavilion

that many Westerners imagine; in fact, it bore more relation to a strict convent school for concubines than a brothel.

Tour highlights

The route of the self-guided tour of the Harem commences at the Carriage Gate, which leads to the Guard Room and Quarters of the Black Eunuchs. The black eunuchs, a group of up to 200 Sudanese slaves, were the only men apart from the sultan allowed to enter the Harem. The next gate, the Cümle

The gilded cage

During the four centuries of Ottoman rule, 80 Ottoman princes, direct descendants of the sultans, were murdered. This was in keeping with Mehmet the Conqueror's decree that the son who inherits the throne should kill his brothers 'in the interests of the world order'.

The record for this mandated fratricide was held by Mehmet III, whose first act as sultan in 1595 was to murder his 19 brothers and dispose of seven concubines who had been impregnated by his father; their bodies were dumped in the Bosphorus.

The Divan became concerned about the extinction of the dynasty, and in 1607 fratricide was replaced with the Cage *(Kafes)* in which male heirs to the throne were kept as pampered prisoners for years – often for life.

Kapısı, opens to the Golden Way, a path of corridors and courtyards that runs from one end of the Harem to the other. Passing the Bath House and the Courtyard of the Concubines, you will reach the Quarters of the Valide Sultan (mother of the ruling sultan), which is strategically located between the apartments of the sultan and his higher-ranking favourites.

Other highlights of the Harem include the Room with Fountains, which Murat III used as a bedroom and for private conversations, turning the taps on to discourage eavesdroppers.

The Sultan's Chamber (Hünkâr Sofrası), the biggest room in the Harem, is where the girls competed for the sultan's attention, dancing and playing musical instruments.

MUSEUM OF ARCHAEOLOGY

Leave the palace and return to the First Court, where you should walk down the hill towards the impressive neoclassical pillared building on the right, the **Museum of Archaeology** ⑬ (Arkeoloji Müzesi; Osman Hamdi Bey Yokuşu; tel: 0212 520 7740; www.istanbularkeolji.gov.tr; Tue–Sun 9am–5pm; charge). Founded in 1881 by Osman Hamdi Bey, one of Turkey's first archaeologists, the museum is a treasure trove of Classical and pre-Classical artefacts.

The first thing you see on entering is the giant contorted face of the Egyptian god Bes, intended to scare away evil

Lions from the Ishtar Gate at Babylon in the Museum of Archaeology

spirits. Also on display are a mummified Egyptian king and Roman statues. Remnants of Byzantine Constantinople include a snake head from the Serpentine Column in the Hippodrome, lions from the 5th-century Bucoleon Palace, and a rare 7th-century mosaic that survived the iconoclastic era in the 8th and 9th centuries. Take a tea-break in the courtyard café.

AROUND GÜLHANE PARK

After your immersion in Ottoman and archaeological history, relax with a stroll under the shade of the giant plane trees that line the paths of **Gülhane Park** ⓮ (Gülhane Parkı), a large and peaceful green space at the base of the palace grounds, just down the hill from the Archaeology Museum.

Exit via the **Çizme Gate** (Çizme Kapısı) at the southern end onto Alemdar Caddesi, and turn right up the cobbled slope of **Soğukçeşme Sokak**. This little street, running between the outer walls of Topkapı Palace and Hagia Sophia, is lined by brightly painted restored Ottoman houses. Here you will find Aya Sofya Mansions as well as **Dervis**, see ❷, set underground in a Byzantine cistern.

Continue to the top of the street to return to the **Fountain of Sultan Ahmet III**. Alternatively, if you are in need of refreshment, take a right onto Caferiye Sokak and right again down the alleyway to the courtyard of the **Caferağa Medresesi**, see ❸. A former religious school built by the architect Sinan in 1559, this blissfully tranquil enclave serves a double purpose as a café and an arts centre; the latter offers courses in everything from calligraphy to porcelain decoration.

Food and Drink

❶ KONYALI RESTAURANT AND CAFÉ

Topkapı Palace Lokantası; tel: 0212 513 9696; www.konyalilokantasi.com; Wed–Mon 8.30am–4.30pm; $$–$$$
This İstanbul institution has had a monopoly on lunch at Topkapı Palace since 1967, serving traditional Turkish cuisine like oven-baked lamb.

❷ DERVIS

Kabasakal Sokak, Sultanahmet; tel: 0212 516 1515; daily B, L and AT; $
A semi-outdoor leafy café, this is a relaxing pit-stop where you can enjoy tea, snacks and nargiles, in full view of the Blue Mosque and its Sound and Light show in the evenings.

❸ CAFERAĞA MEDRESESI

Caferiye Sokak Soğukkuyu Çıkmazı 1; tel: 0212 513 3601/02; daily 8.30am–4pm; $
Built in 1559 for Caferağa, a eunuch during the reign of Süleyman the Magnificent, this former *medrese* serves basic Turkish fare in a pretty, peaceful courtyard.

Nuruosmaniye Gate

THE GRAND BAZAAR

Constructed by Mehmet the Conqueror, for centuries the Grand Bazaar was the hub of oriental trade routes. Lose yourself among its labyrinthine alleyways and courtyards, historic merchants' houses and mosques.

DISTANCE: 1.5km (1 mile)
TIME: 3 hours
START: Nuruosmaniye Caddesi
END: Çorlulu Ali Paşa Medresesi
POINTS TO NOTE: The bazaar is a short uphill walk from Sultanahmet, or you can take the tram to Çemberlitaş and walk up Vezirhan Caddesi to join Nuruosmaniye Caddesi. Three hours should give you a good feel for the bazaar and its highlights, although shopaholics could easily spend the day here. The bazaar is closed on Sundays.

Although the shops are now mainly geared towards tourists, the Grand Bazaar still retains a great deal of its oriental flavour in the blackened corners and arched courtyards of its *hans* (merchants' inns), as well as in the workshops and stalls of traditional blacksmiths and bronzesmiths, jew-

ellers and fabric merchants, miniature painters and antiques dealers.

It is as easy to lose track of time in this covered labyrinth as it is to lose oneself in its hectic, meandering alleyways. Don't be afraid to put the map away, as part of the fun is getting lost, although making your way through the crowds amid the persistent cajoling of shopkeepers can take its toll.

NURUOSMANIYE CADDESI

The wider bazaar district stretches all the way down the hill to the Golden

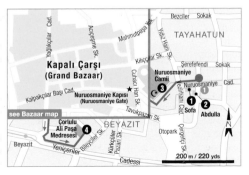

Scarves edged with coins

Old Bedestan entrance

Horn at Eminönü, and many of these little streets, awash with İstanbullus haggling for clothing or kitchenware, are also worth exploring.

Begin a little way to the east on **Nuruosmaniye Caddesi**, a pedestrianised shopping street that leads past the mosque of the same name and into the bazaar. Look for **Kashif Sofa ❶** (no. 53; tel: 0212 520 2850), with an eclectic range of antique artefacts, copperware, calligraphy, paintings and contemporary art. Just around the corner, on Ali Baba Türbe Sokak, is **Abdulla ❼**, specialising in *hamam* wares, such as silk and cotton *pestemals* (*hamam* towels), natural olive-oil soap and wooden *hamam* shoes, and beautiful, finely-woven silk shawls. The shop is within the chic café, **Fes**, see ❶, great for coffee or lunch. There's another branch in the bazaar, see ❷.

Nuruosmaniye Mosque

Continue west along Nuruosmaniye Caddesi until you reach the pleasant horseshoe-shaped courtyard of the **Nuruosmaniye Mosque ❸** (Nuruosmaniye Camii). Completed in 1755 by Osman III, its avant-garde Baroque style was disapproved of by the Islamic clergy of the time.

Leave the courtyard and enter the bazaar through the **Nuruosmaniye Gate ❹** (Nuruosmaniye Kapısı), where you will emerge right in the thick of it on the main drag, Kalpakcılar Caddesi, just south of the gates of the **Sandal Bedesteni ❸**.

THE GRAND BAZAAR

With 66 narrow streets housing more than 4,000 shops, as well as banks, cafés, restaurants, mosques, a *hamam* and even a chaotic **stock exchange ❻**, the **Grand Bazaar** (Kapali Carşi; open Mon–Sat 9am–7pm) is the world's largest covered market, with up to 40,000 visitors a day passing through each of its main entrance gates.

Layout

At the heart of the bazaar is the **Old Bazaar ❹** (İç Bedesten). Formerly a secure storeroom (*bedesten*), its original domed structure has remained

Getting the price right

A source of excitement to some and an ignominious process for others: whether you like it or not, haggling is an intrinsic part of shopping in the bazaar. There are very few traders who are not willing to shift on their marked prices, and to get the best deal you will need time on your hands and the capacity to drink countless cups of tea. In the process of bartering, start by cutting the asking price down by half (never quote a price you don't want to pay), then meet somewhere in the middle with the trader. Never feel pressured to buy, don't be afraid to walk away, and always make sure you are happy with the agreed price before parting with your cash.

Tailor at work in one of the hans

intact for over five centuries. Today, the hall contains jewellery and antiques shops that sell everything from Ottoman swords to Russian icons. There's also a chance to stop for a bite to eat at the **Bedesten Café & Patisserie**, see ❸.

The rest of the Grand Bazaar is roughly divided into sections: the areas directly surrounding the northern and southern sides of the Old Bazaar hold antiques and carpet shops; the eastern section of the market is dominated by gold and silversmiths; the western side is known for its leather and copper merchants. The other portions are dotted with shops selling ceramics, pashminas (the quality varies wildly), lanterns, *nargiles* and inlaid backgammon sets.

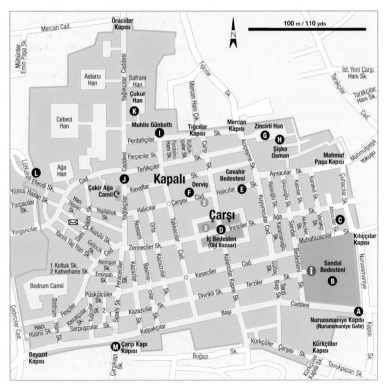

Lamps for sale   *Backgammon boards*

Halıcılar Sokak

Directly north of the Old Bazaar is **Halıcılar Sokak** ⑤, traditionally the street of the carpet dealers. It's a lively place lined with a handful of cafés and quirky shops like **Derviş** ⑥ (www.dervis.com). Purveyor of ethnic shirts, dresses and even dowry cloths, this little store is a textile-lover's fantasy, as well as a respected merchant of *hamam* supplies.

Zincirli Han

From here, head up towards the northeastern corner of the market to the delightful, leafy **Zincirli Han** ⑥, one of many hans dotted around the periphery of the bazaar. Usually centred around a courtyard, these inns from the former days of the Silk Road are spread over two colonnaded levels, and are now mostly occupied by workshops.

Zincirli Han, once the domain of the chain-makers, is home to one of the most prominent carpet dealers, **Şişko Osman** ⑪ (www.siskoosman.com).

Directly west from here is Perdahcılar Sokak and **Muhlis Günbattı** ⑪, who stocks a fascinating collection of Anatolian and Central Asian fabrics and items of clothing that are popular with local collectors. At the end of the passage is **Yağlıkçılar Caddesi** ⑪, one of the bazaar's main arteries.

Çukur Han

Turning right here will take you towards quiet **Çukur Han** ⑯, home to **Dalida Ceramics**.

Lütfullah Efendi Sokak

Now head back into the fray, south then west through the leather and denim section to a far-flung western corner of the bazaar. The outlying **Lütfullah Efendi Sokak** ⑪ is a tranquil courtyard occupied by veteran **Tuğra Bakır**, a copper merchant with handmade and engraved jugs, plates and lamps.

Leave the bazaar through the **Çarşı Kapı Gate** ⑯, head down the street and turn left onto Yeniçeriler Caddesi and left again into the **Çorlulu Ali Paşa Medresesi** ④. A former religious school, it now has a *nargile courtyard café*.

Food and Drink

① & ② FES CAFÉ

Nuruosmaniye, Ali Baba Türbe Sokak 25–27; tel: 0212 526 3070; Mon–Sat 9am–7pm; $$
This café serves basic breakfast and lunch fare (sandwiches and salads), as well as different blends of tea and coffee, and fresh lemonade. There's another branch inside the Grand Bazaar.

③ BEDESTEN CAFÉ & PATISSERIE

İç Bedesten (Old Bazaar) 143–151; tel: 0212 520 2250; Mon–Sat 9am–7pm; $
The scenic surroundings of this café are a great option for a spot of mid-shopping refuelling. Grab a quick sandwich or linger over a coffee and *fırın sütlaç* (traditional rice pudding) on elegant red leather couches.

EMINÖNÜ

Steer your way through the crowds of fishermen on the Galata Bridge, shop with the locals in Eminönü's chaotic network of bazaars, and finish off with a nostalgic evocation of the era of the Orient Express.

DISTANCE: 2km (1.25 miles)
TIME: 2–3 hours
START: Galata Bridge, north side
END: Sirkeci Train Station
POINTS TO NOTE: It is best to do this tour on a weekday, as the Saturday shopping crowd can render Eminönü's tiny backstreets impassable and the shops close on Sundays. To start from the Beyoğlu side of the Galata Bridge, take the tram to the Karaköy stop and walk from there.

Located at the mouth of the Golden Horn, İstanbul's natural harbour, Eminönü has been the centre of the city's port and commercial activity for centuries. The wares brought ashore from cargo ships gave rise to the Egyptian Bazaar and the warren of markets in the surrounding backstreets.

At rush hour the waterfront becomes a bedlam of bodies as commuters pour off the ferries from Beyoğlu or the Asian side, and the air is loud with blasts from ships' horns.

GALATA BRIDGE

Cross the **Galata Bridge** ❶ (Galata Köprüsü), the main artery that connects Ottoman-era İstanbul with the more modern neighbourhoods of Galata and Beyoğlu on the northern side. The first bridge here was a wooden structure, built in 1845. It was replaced in 1910 by the famous old pontoon bridge with its seafood restaurants, until it burned down and was replaced by the present bridge in 1992.

Walking across the bridge from north to south affords a superb panorama of the Old City's minaret-pierced skyline and the scores of fishermen here from dawn 'til dusk. To cross the busy road to the south of the bridge, you will need to descend into the **underground walkway**, packed with shops and vendors. Keep a hand on your wallet.

EMINÖNÜ'S BACKSTREETS

You will emerge on **Eminönü Square** (Eminönü Meydanı), dominated by the New Mosque to the left. Cross over, fol-

low the edge of the Egyptian Bazaar, which juts into the square, and then turn right along the row of vegetable stalls on Kalçin Sokak. Walk to the end, where you will see a small alleyway on the left called Kızılhan Sokağı.

This alleyway, with its sackcloth merchants and paper-napkin suppliers, is framed by centuries-old market buildings that stretch off into other alleyways and arched courtyards.

Rüstem Paşa Mosque

Turn right on to Hasırcılar Caddesi and after a few metres you will see a stone archway on the right with steps lead-

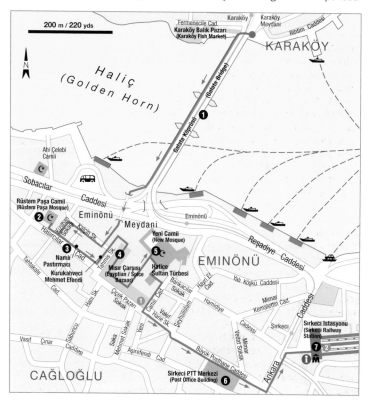

New Mosque

ing up to the **Rüstem Paşa Mosque**
❷ (Rüstem Paşa Camii). This small,
hidden-away mosque was built by
Mimar Sinan in 1561 to commemorate Rüstem Paşa, twice a grand vizier
under Süleyman the Magnificent and
husband of the sultan's favourite
daughter, Mihrimah Sultan. Built on a
terrace above a complex of shops (the
rent from these used to go towards the
msoque's upkeep), Rüstem Paşa is
notable for its spectacular İznik tiles,
some coloured with shades that were
never again reproduced in İznik kilns.

HASIRCILAR CADDESI

Turn left into tarpaulin-covered **Hasırcılar Caddesi** ❸, one of Eminönü's
busiest shopping streets. Here, amid the
throngs, you will find shops and stands
selling kitchenware, mobile phones and
party decorations, as well as cheese,
nuts, dried fruit, kebabs and freshly
squeezed orange juice.

As you negotiate your way, look for
Namlı Pastırmacı (www.namlipas
tirma.com.tr) on the left at nos 14–16.
This colourful eat-in and take-away deli
is packed with Turkish specialities, pick-
led, stuffed, baked or fried. Hasırcılar
Caddesi leads to the Egyptian Bazaar,
but first turn left on Tahmis Sokak,
where, at no. 66, Turkish coffee aficio-
nados will love the old-fashioned industrial coffee grinders at **Kurukahveci
Mehmet Efendi** (www.mehmetefendi.
com). It's the most popular place in the
area to buy freshly ground coffee – by
the bag or in a box.

EGYPTIAN BAZAAR

Enter the **Egyptian Bazaar** ❹ (Mısır
Çarşısı, also known as the Spice Bazaar;
Mon–Sat 8am–6pm) from the north-
ernmost entrance, where Tahmis Sokak
meets the square in front of the New
Mosque. The bazaar was built in 1664
as part of the New Mosque complex; its
name derives from the goods once sold
here, having arrived by sea via the annual
'Cairo Caravan'. The brick walls and high,
vaulted ceilings give it all the allure of the
Grand Bazaar, but at a fraction of the size.

The bazaar's stalls brim with heaps
of herbs, spices, tea leaves, nuts and
lokum (Turkish Delight), as well as
honey, olive oil and caviar, and even the
odd pot of the aphrodisiac 'Turkish Via-
gra'. Also peppered around are stalls
selling natural soaps and sponges,
ceramics, jewellery and scarves. Used
to a steady influx of tourists, the vendors can be tiresome and their prices
often inordinately high. But try the **Ari-
foğlu Spice Centre** at stall no. 59, a
no-hassle trader with a wide stock of
medicinal herbs and oils.

To leave, take the exit in the middle
of the bazaar that leads out into the
plant and pet market. Here dogs, ducks,
pheasants, rabbits and even leeches
are available to buy, but you will most
likely prefer to take a breather in one of
the adjacent **open-air cafés**.

Spices in the Egyptian Bazaar

Friday prayers at the New Mosque

NEW MOSQUE

The **New Mosque** ❺ (Yeni Camii) is an ideal place to observe the workings of a large neighbourhood mosque in regular use by worshippers. Due to power shifts in the sultanate and consequent funding problems, the mosque's construction dragged on for several decades. It was finally completed in 1663 under the supervision of Mehmet IV's mother, the Valide Turhan Hatice. Her **tomb** (Hatice Sultan Türbesi; daily 9.30am–4.30pm; free) is opposite the mosque.

Something of a permanent fixture at the mosque is its massive pigeon population, which swarms over the square in front. Special stands set up by the municipality sell pigeon food.

Lunch option

For a meal in scenic surroundings, enter the Egyptian Bazaar at the Yeni Camii Caddesi entrance and find the obscured entrance on the left-hand side of the gateway, where steps lead up to the charming **Bab-ı Hayat**, see ❶.

SIRKECI TRAIN STATION

Now make your way east down Vakıf Hane Sokak, which turns into Büyük Posthane Caddesi. You will pass the grandiose late-Ottoman **Post Office Building** ❻ (Sirkeci PTT Merkezi) on your right (pop in for a look at the giant portrait of Atatürk and the stained-glass ceiling in the main hall).

Turn left on Ankara Caddesi, and after a couple of blocks is the entrance to **Sirkeci Station** ❼ (Sirkeci Istasyonu). Erected in 1890, this was once the terminus of the Orient Express train service, although today the station only serves a handful of foreign destinations and the city's suburbs. Its former glamour can be glimpsed in the stained-glass windows and chandeliers of its waiting rooms and restaurant, the **Orient Express**, see ❷. A small **museum** (Tue–Sat 9am–5pm; free) houses nostalgic rail mementos.

Food and Drink

❶ BAB-I HAYAT

Egyptian Bazaar (above the Haseki Gate), Yeni Camii Caddesi 39–47; 0212 520 7878; www.babihayat.com; daily 8am–7.30pm; $$

With its hand-painted domed ceilings and coloured tiled walls, Bab-ı Hayat is perfect for a quiet lunch far from the madding crowds below. The Turkish fare is served *à la carte* or canteen-style.

❷ ORIENT EXPRESS RESTAURANT

Sirkeci Station, Istasyon Caddesi; tel: 0212 522 2280; daily 11.30am–midnight; $$

A veteran of the early days of the Republic, abuzz with artists and the literati in the 1950s and 60s, this restaurant is a shadow of its former self. It serves Turkish classics like kebabs, fava beans with lamb, and shrimp casserole.

Galata skyline from Eminönü

GALATA, TÜNEL & PERA

Home to İstanbul's cool bohemians and café crawlers, these three interwoven neighbourhoods are a maze of cobbled backstreets, whirling with restaurants, bars and boutiques and even the odd Dervish.

DISTANCE: 2km (1.25 miles)
TIME: A half day
START: Karaköy Fish Market
END: 360 restaurant
POINTS TO NOTE: Aim to do this tour during the afternoon, as the view from the Galata Tower is at its most sublime around sunset, and early evening is when the cafés and bars in Tünel come to life. To access the starting point, alight at Karaköy tram stop.

GALATA

The northern shore of the Golden Horn was traditionally the quarter where craftsmen, foreign merchants and diplomats made their homes, beginning in the 11th century when the Genoese founded a trading colony in the district of Galata. Following the conquest, European ambassadors built their mansions on the hills beyond Galata, a place which came to be called Pera (Greek for 'beyond'). Foreigners from the entire Ottoman Empire flooded into Galata and Pera, attracted by the wealth and sophistication of the capital. As the area became crowded, the wealthy foreign merchants and diplomats moved further along the Grande

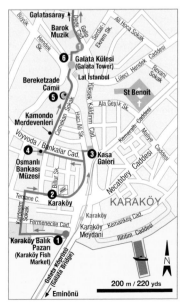

Karaköy Fish Market   *Meyhane on Sofyalı Sokak*

Rue de Pera (now İstiklal Caddesi), forming a focus for the 19th- and 20th-century expansion of the modern, European-style part of İstanbul, known as Beyoğlu.

Once known for its taverns and ribald entertainment, Galata underwent a renaissance in the early 20th century, when a fresh wave of foreigners inundated the city by way of the Orient Express. Now cafés, bars and clubs catering to the city's bohemian youth have sprung up within the previously dilapidated buildings.

Karaköy Fish Market

The **Karaköy Fish Market ❶** (Karaköy Balık Pazarı; daily dawn until dusk) is located at the foot of the Galata Bridge on the northwestern side. This collection of open-air stalls sells fish so fresh that many are still flipping their tails. The little waterside park at the end of the market houses a couple of small ramshackle cafés that grill the market fish on the spot and serve them on bread or with salad.

The area close to the mouth of the Golden Horn is filled with hardware stores. Pass up from the park though Kardeşim Sokak, turn right on Tersane Caddesi and head towards the entrance to the **funicular railway ❷** on your left.

Bank Street

Veer left up the hill towards Bankalar Caddesi (also known as Voyvoda Cad-

desi), the centre of banking during imperial days. Art lovers could drop by the **Kasa Galeri ❸** at no. 2 (tel: 0212 292 4939; http://kasagaleri.sabanciuniv. edu; Mon–Sat 10am–5.30pm; free), a contemporary art space run by Sabancı University. Otherwise, continue to no. 11, where the former **Ottoman Bank Building** has been transformed into a **museum ❹** (Osmanlı Bankası Müzesi; tel: 0212 334 2200; www.obmuze.com; Tue–Sat noon–8pm, Sun until 6pm; charge), chronicling the financial institution's role as the central bank and treasury of the Ottoman Empire.

From the Bank Museum, cross the road, turn into Camekan Sokak and start your climb up the hill, passing the elaborate 19th-century **Camondo Steps** (Kamondo Merdevenleri), donated to the neighbourhood by the wealthy Ottoman-Jewish Camondo family of bankers and philanthropists.

Bereketzade Mosque

About two-thirds of the way along, take a break from the uphill hike to look at the pint-sized **Bereketzade Mosque ❺** (Bereketzade Camii), which has recently been restored to its former glory. It was originally constructed in 1453 by Haci Ali Bereketzade, the keeper of the Galata Tower. It is said that there is a man-sized passage that runs from the Galata Tower to the mosque and all the way down to Karaköy Harbour.

There are some small boutiques at the top of Camekan Sokak, includ-

Architectural detail, Tünel Square

ing **Lal İstanbul** (tel: 0212 293 2571; www.lalistanbul.com) at no. 14. This family-run shop specialises in quirky handmade items, such as leather goods, jewellery and T-shirts.

Galata Tower

Looming ahead is the giant cylindrical **Galata Tower** ➌ (Galata Külesi; tel: 0212 293 8180; daily 9am–8pm; charge), built by Genoese settlers in 1348 to defend their colony. The viewing gallery is 61m (200ft) above ground (relax – there's a lift), and the 360-degree panorama it affords is certainly worth the entrance fee. New restaurants have sprung up around the square in which the tower sits; the most boisterous of these is **Enginar**, see ➊.

Music shops

At the top of the square turn right and take the first left up Galip Dede Caddesi, where a clutch of shops specialise in musical instruments. At **Barok Muzik** (no. 64) the gregarious owner sells and gives lessons in every kind of old-fashioned Turkish instrument, from *darbuka* and *bendir* drums to the stringed *ud* and *bağlama*.

Galata Dervish Lodge

At the top of Galip Dede Caddesi is the **Galata Dervish Lodge** ➐ (Galata Mevlevihanesi, Galip Dede Caddesi 15; tel: 0212 245 4141; www.galatamevlevihanesimuzesi.gov.tr) the first of its kind to be built in İstanbul. Its quiet courtyard and graveyard back onto the *semahane*, the traditional location of the Whirling Dervish ceremonies (see box).

TÜNEL

Take the next left to **Tünel Square** ➑ (Tünel Meydanı), where there's a tram stop and **funicular** station. To explore Tünel's idiosyncratic backstreets, head into the pretty iron-clad **Tünel Arcade** (Tünel Geçisi) opposite. The tables and

---

Whirling Dervishes

Unlike the tacky spectacle of belly dancing, which only continues in İstanbul for dinner-and-show tourist packages, the *sema* (dance) of the Whirling Dervishes is a true Turkish tradition – a meditative journey towards truth and perfection. It survives to this day, despite the banning of the Dervishes and closing down of their lodges in 1923 in accordance with the new laws of the secular Republic. Fortunately, the Sufis managed to preserve their practice under the auspices of a cultural organisation. The white-robed performers can be seen at the Galata Dervish Lodge (Sun 5pm), Hocapaşa Art and Cultural Centre near the station (Mon, Wed, Fri, Sat and Sun 7pm) and in a grand hall at Sirkeci Station (Mon and Fri 7.30pm). Call 0216 349 1114 for details.

Galata Tower

chairs of this plant-filled open-air courtyard belong to **KV**, see ❷. Stop for a coffee, or peruse the antiques and curios in **Artrium** at no. 7 (tel: 0212 251 4302; www.artrium.com.tr) next door. Upon leaving the passage, to your right you will see **Badehane**, see ❸, a legendary social spot.

Head straight ahead (north) along Sofayalı Sokak, making a brief detour at the second left along Şehbender Sokak to check out the schedule of another of the district's renowned establishments, the nightclub and concert venue **Babylon** ❾ (tel: 0212 292 73 68; www.babylon.com.tr). Sofayalı Sokak is filled with laid-back watering holes, restaurants and *meyhanes*. Towards the top is **Refik**, see ❹, Tünel's most popular *meyhane*.

PERA

Turn left into Asmalı Mescit Caddesi and walk downhill until you are confronted with the side façade of the **Pera Palace Hotel** ❿ (tel: 0212 377 4000; www.jumeirah.com; see also page 104). An icon since the early days of the Republic, the hotel was popular in the 1920s with the travellers who came to the city aboard the Orient Express. Among them were Agatha Christie, Ernest Hemingway, Leon Trotsky and Mata Hari.

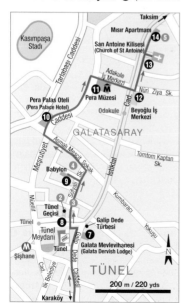

Pera Museum

Walk north up Meşrutiyet Caddesi until you reach, at no. 65, the **Pera Museum** ⓫ (Pera Müzesi; tel: 0212 334 9900; www.peramuzesi.org.tr; Tue–Sat 10am–7pm, Sun noon–6pm; charge), which exhibits a curious but attractive combination of Ottoman paintings and Anatolian weights and measures, along with temporary exhibitions, usually of contemporary art.

Just after the museum, to the right, is a small passage called Odakule İş Merkezi, which will eject you into the crowd on the main thoroughfare of İstiklal Caddesi (see also page 58). Opposite are the discounted clothes stalls of the **Beyoğlu İş Merkezi** ⓬.

Ottoman painting at the Pera Museum

Church of St Antoine

Turn left and head north, looking right to see the early 20th-century neo-Gothic **Church of St Antoine** ⑬ (San Antoine Kilisesi; İstiklal Caddesi 325) set in a gated courtyard just off the main street. This is the largest and busiest Catholic church in İstanbul.

Contemporary art and cocktails

Head for the elegant Old Pera-style **Mısır Apartmanı building** ⑭ at no. 163. Treat yourself to one of the coolest cocktails in town by taking the lift to the top floor of the building, which is the location of the **360** restaurant and bar, see ⑤.

Food and Drink

① ENGINAR

Sah Kapısı Sokak 4/A, Galata; tel: 0212 251 7321; Tue–Sun 10.30am–midnight; $$

Enginar serves a selection of simple international dishes. There's indoor and outdoor seating, and live piano and guitar music on Friday and Saturday evenings.

② KV

Tünel Geçisi 10, Tünel; tel: 0212 251 4338; www.kv.com.tr; daily 8am–2am; $$

Set among the coloured lights and thick foliage of the Tünel Arcade, this is an elegant bistro-style restaurant by night and a popular café by day. The menu features soups, salads and house specials, including traditional Turkish dishes like the Imperial Kebab (made with veal) and a dessert of figs soaked in cognac.

③ BADEHANE

General Yazgan Sokak 5, Tünel; tel: 0212 249 0550; daily 9am–2am; $

You might have to wait for a place at this popular neighbourhood watering hole, where tables and chairs spill casually into the street outside and local bohemians sip on glasses of Efes beer. Badehane comes alive on Wednesday nights, when local Roma music luminary Selim Sesler performs a set.

④ REFIK

Sofyalı Sokak 10–12, Tünel; tel: 0212 243 2834; www.refikrestaurant.com; Mon–Sat noon–midnight; $$

A true İstanbul institution, Refik offers *meze*, fish and *rakı* à la carte or as part of a fixed menu. In good weather, get a table outside for the best atmosphere.

⑤ 360

Mısır Apartmanı, İstiklal Caddesi 163; tel: 0212 251 1042; www.360istanbul.com; Sun–Fri noon–2.30am, Sat noon–4am; $$$

Join the city's in-crowd at this so-hip-it-hurts top-floor restaurant and bar. Pop in for a cocktail and soak up the incredible view from their terrace, or stay for dinner and late-night dancing with a DJ.

**İSTİKLAL
CADDESİ   1 ⟵⟶ 265**

TOMTOM MAHALLESİ

BEYOĞLU

The main promenade

TAKSİM TO TOPHANE

Join the flurry of shoppers on Beyoğlu's main promenade, İstiklal Caddesi, then slip into a side street for a great choice of cafés and restaurants. Change gear in the quiet districts of Çukurcuma and Cihangir, then descend to Tophane for contemporary art at İstanbul Modern.

DISTANCE: 3km (2 miles)
TIME: A half day
START: Taksim Square
END: Tophane nargile cafés
POINTS TO NOTE: If you choose to do the route in the afternoon, you could do it in reverse order to end up at İstiklal Caddesi in the evening for dining and Taksim at night for clubbing. Alternatively, take the tram from Tophane to Kabataş and ascend to Taksim via the funicular.

Clubbing

With international DJs, energetic clientele and late-night opening, Taksim's nightclubs are a partygoer's dream. Jazz joints, karaoke bars, live concert venues and house and techno clubs – Beyoğlu's backstreets buzz with nightlife opportunities.

A far cry from the Old City, Taksim is the hub of İstanbul's modern life. Youth culture anchored in European customs has flourished, with the springing up of bars, nightclubs, cinemas, shops and tattoo parlours. Come on any weekday and the main pedestrian strip, İstiklal Caddesi, will be buzzing; come at the weekend and you might need to shoulder your way through the hordes.

The neighbourhoods of Çukurcuma and Cihangir, which lie below Taksim and the top half of İstiklal Caddesi, are quiet by comparison. Largely residential, but with some great local shops and cafés, they are favourites with the arty-liberal home crowd and İstanbul's ex-pat population.

A short walk down the hill will take you to Tophane and the İstanbul Modern, a former dockside warehouse where you can see some of the best Turkish art from the last century, before relaxing with a *nargile* at one of Tophane's outdoor smoking joints.

TAKSIM SQUARE

With a Metro station, tram stop, funicular railway, bus terminal and enormous traffic roundabout, there is never a dull or quiet moment in **Taksim Square ❶** (Taksim Meydanı), consid-

Fish Market entrance

ered to be the city centre. The plaza is named after the 275-year-old cistern on its western side, which is primed to open as the **Republic Museum** (Cumhuriyet Müzesi), documenting İstanbul's part in the formation of the Republic.

İSTIKLAL CADDESI

Head down **İstiklal Caddesi**, which commences from Taksim Square's southwestern corner. Once called the Grand Rue de Pera, this pedestrianised street was renamed 'Independence Street' in 1923, after the formation of the Republic. Nevertheless, the street's architecture still reflects its origins as the main street in İstanbul's late 19th-century European quarter. Restored trams trundle up and down its length every few minutes.

Side streets
The side streets that lead off both sides of İstiklal Caddesi contain a mind-boggling array of cafés, restaurants and bars. To get a taste

of these areas, take the second right into Zambak Sokak, then turn left into Kurabiye Sokak, where you will find the vegetarian restaurant **Zencefil**, see

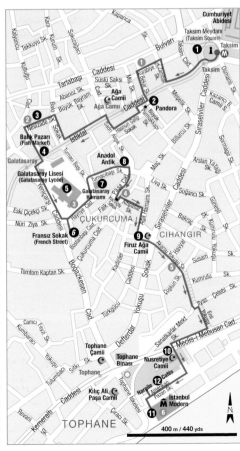

Tram on İstiklal Caddesi

page 114. Take another left into Bekar Sokak, passing the fantastic Turkish grill **Zübeyir**, see ❶.

Regain İstiklal Caddesi for a short way, then take the second left into Büyük Parmakkapı Sokak. To your left is **Pandora** ❷, an excellently stocked bookshop with a whole floor devoted to English-language books. Now turn right into Hasnun Galip Sokak and right again into Sadri Alışık Sokak to return to the main street. On the corner directly opposite is İstiklal stalwart **Hacı Abdullah**, see page 112.

Nevizade Sokak

Continue down the street for a couple of blocks until you reach Balo Sokak to your right, home to a batch of clubs and bars, and take a left into **Nevizade Sokak** ❸. This recently spruced-up alley is packed with *meyhanes*, local restaurants in the mould of traditional Greek tavernas (see page 16). It is best returned to at night, when crowds of diners fill the tables, the rakı and beer flow freely, and giant trays of fresh *meze* make the rounds. **İmroz**, see page 112, is a good option here for eating; for late-night drinks and music, try **Gızlı Bahçe**, see ❷.

Fish Market

Make a left at the end of Nevizade Sokak for another food-related treat in the form of the **Fish Market** ❹ (Balık Pazarı). This bustling arcade has a wide selection of piscine delights for sale, as well as other, albeit rather expensive, food shops.

Galatasaray Lycée

Back on İstiklal Caddesi, cross over towards the large outer walls of the **Galatasaray Lycée** ❺ (Galatasaray Lisesi), the oldest high school in the city, which started life in 1481 as the Galata Palace Imperial School. Take a left here onto Yeniçarşı Caddesi and walk around the lycée until you reach Hayriye Caddesi, which curves to the left. Here **Cezayir**, see ❸, is a former 19th-century school converted into a restaurant and bar, with a beautiful summer garden round the back.

It's a better option for a drink or bite to eat than the glut of newly built establishments on adjacent **French Street** ❻ (Fransız Sokak). Also known as Cezayir Sokak, this steep little street is a curious replication of a bistro-filled Parisian alley.

ÇUKURCUMA

Continue to the end of Hayriye Caddesi, and take the steps that go left up Çapanoğlu Sokak, leading up the hill past the **Galatasaray Hamam** ❼ (see page 23) on the left. From the baths, take a right into Turnacıbaşı Sokak.

This street marks the centre of **Çukurcuma**, a neighbourhood known for the antiques shops that populate its sooty and gloomy backstreets. One of the largest, at no. 65, is **Anadol Antik** ❽,

Vintage accessories, Çukurcuma

a treasure house of furniture and artefacts from the late Ottoman era and early days of the Republic.

The antiques shops continue along Faik Paşa Caddesi, a street lined with once majestic, now somewhat down-at-heel, late 19th-century apartment buildings. From this street, take a left into Hacioğlu Sokak, home to **Çukurcuma Köftecisi** and its delicious grilled meatballs, see ❹. The street leads to a small square; throw a glance right towards the picturesque **Muhyiddin Molla Fenari Mosque** (Muhyiddin Molla Fenari Camii), but turn left then immediately right up the hill along Altıpatlar Sokak.

Up in smoke

Also known as a *shisha*, hubble-bubble or hookah, the *nargile* continues to be a long-standing Turkish tradition, despite the Western trend for banning smoking in cafés and restaurants. Scores of specialist cafés stock racks of these smoking instruments, which burn thick, sticky molasses in all kinds of flavours (apple, cherry, coconut, cappuccino, cola – you name it). The essential accompaniments to any good *nargile* are copious glasses of *çayı* and a drawn-out game of *tavla* (backgammon). Not just an old man's habit, nargiles are increasingly popular with young people, and women in particular.

CİHANGİR

Turn right into Ağa Hamamı Sokak and follow it up until you see the **Firuz Ağa Mosque** ❾ (Firuz Ağa Camii), facing out onto Sıraselviler Caddesi and enlivened by the ever-popular café **Firuz Ağa** (tel: 0212 243 2914). This is the heart of Cihangir.

Head down Akarsu Yokuşu Caddesi for more café-bistros, the hang-outs of the artists, actors and writers who live in the surrounding streets. One such joint is **Smyrna** at no. 29, see ❺. At the end of Akarsu Yokuşu Caddesi is a flight of steps set into the steep hill that descends to the Bosphorus. Walk down here and bear left when you reach Ilyas Çelebi Sokak to find the final set of steps on Enli Yokuşu.

TOPHANE

You are now entering Tophane, where one of its waterside warehouses has been converted into a major art space.

İstanbul Modern

Take a right along the busy Meclisi Mebusan Caddesi and cross over when you see the signs for the İstanbul Modern, just before the elaborate Baroque exterior of the **Nusretiye Mosque** ❿ (Nusretiye Camii). Not visible from the street, the museum is nestled at the end of a car park on the water's edge.

Opened in 2004, the **İstanbul Modern** ⓫ (Meclisi Mebusan Caddesi;

İstanbul Modern

tel: 0212 334 7300; www.istanbul modern.org; Tue–Wed and Fri–Sun 10am–6pm, Thur 10am–8pm; charge) has fast become a city institution. The first floor houses contemporary art shows, installations and video projections, while on the second floor there's a permanent exhibition of 20th-century Turkish art, including lithographs by Hoca Ali Rıza and paintings by Şeker Ahmet Paşa. The museum's

chic **café**, see ⑥, has a fantastic view of the Bosphorus.

You could finish your tour by enjoying a quiet moment the local way – over a *nargile* (see box). The row of **nargile cafés** ⑫ at Tophane (accessible via the gateway next to the car park entrance) are among the most popular with young people, who while away the hours with a pipe in one hand and backgammon dice in the other.

Food and Drink

① ZÜBEYIR
Bekar Sokak 28, Beyoğlu; tel: 0212 293 3951; daily noon–3am; $$
This Taksim staple offers top-quality kebabs and grilled meat over its two floors. Garden in summer.

② GIZLI BAHÇE
Nevizade Sokak 27, Beyoğlu; tel: 0212 249 2192; daily noon–2am; $$
A low-key bar with a quirky interior, which gets pretty noisy on Friday and Saturday nights.

③ CEZAYIR
Hayriye Caddesi 16, Beyoğlu; tel: 0212 245 9980; www.cezayir-istanbul.com; daily 10am–2am; $$$
A restaurant, café and bar rolled into one. The modern Turkish menu features sea bass ceviche and steamed anchovies with cracked wheat pilaf.

④ ÇUKURCUMA KÖFTECISI
Hacıoğlu Sokak 1/A, Çukurcuma; tel: 0212 245 0833; www.cukurcumakoftecisi.com; Sun–Fri noon–6pm, Sat until 8pm; $–$$
You will smell the *köfte* and home-made stews before you reach this great neighbourhood joint.

⑤ SMYRNA
Akarsu Yokuşu Caddesi 29, Cihangir; tel: 0212 244 2466; daily 10am–2am; $$–$$$
Cihangir's trendiest hang-out, this cosy café is good for everything from brunch to late-night drinks.

⑥ ISTANBUL MODERN CAFÉ
İstanbul Modern; tel: 0212 292 2612; www.istanbulmodern.org; daily 10am–midnight; $$$
Enjoy lunch, dinner or just a coffee on the waterfront. The menu includes spicy octopus with apple and black cabbage stuffed with minced meat.

Dolmabahçe Palace

DOLMABAHÇE TO ORTAKÖY

Immerse yourself in the Baroque recesses of the last Ottoman palace of Dolmabahçe, drop anchor at the Naval Museum at Beşiktaş, stroll around picturesque Yıldız Park, and finish your day with a waterside dinner in Ortaköy.

DISTANCE: 5.25km (3.25 miles)
TIME: A leisurely day
START: Kabataş tram stop
END: Ortaköy Square
POINTS TO NOTE: This isn't always the most picturesque of walks, and although parallel to the Bosphorus it's rarely in view. But as a route to link up places of interest, it can't be beaten. Bear in mind that the Dolmabahçe Palace is closed on Monday and Thursday.

The section of the Bosphorus shore stretching from Kabataş to Ortaköy boasts some of the best examples of late Ottoman architecture from the 18th and 19th centuries. Foremost is the majestic Dolmabahçe Palace, which was built beside the water at great expense for a sultanate determined to break with the past and mod-

ernise in a 'civilised' European manner. Thus its elaborate façade has more affinity with Versailles than with the domes and arches of Topkapı, and this French château style of architecture is echoed in the nearby Cirağan and Yıldız palaces.

DOLMABAHÇE PALACE

Begin at Kabataş, where there is a bus and ferry terminal, as well as a tram stop and a funicular train to Taksim

Luxurious Palace furnishings   *On the waterfront at Beşiktaş*

Square, making this area one of the city's best-served transport hubs. Walk north for a few minutes to reach the single-domed neo-Baroque **Dolmabahçe Mosque ❶** (Dolmabahçe Camii, Meclisi Mebusan Caddesi; daily 9am–6pm; free), which was built for the sultans in 1851. It's a few minutes' walk further on in the same direction to the imposing grounds of **Dolmabahçe Palace ❷** (Dolmabahçe Sarayı; tel: 0212 236 9000; Tue–Wed and Fri–Sun 9am–4pm; guided tours only; charge).

A white elephant

Mahmud II (1808–39) had already abandoned the ageing Topkapı Palace for various Bosphorus residences (which no longer exist), but it was his son Abdül Mecit who was responsible for constructing Dolmabahçe in the mid-19th century. However, although the palace was meant to be a statement of the sultan's faith in the future of his empire, it turned out to be a monument to folly and extravagance. Its construction nearly emptied the imperial treasury, and the running costs contributed to the empire's bankruptcy in 1875. Following the creation of the Republic in 1923, the palace was used by Mustafa Atatürk as the official presidential residence. He died here in 1938 (see page 64).

Palace interior

The palace can only be seen on a guided tour, which is split into two parts: the first visits the Selamlik, the public wing, while the second covers the Harem. If you are short of time, more worthwhile is the **Selamlık**. Here, the ornate, curved staircase that leads to the **Salon of the Ambassadors**, the imperial reception room, is jaw-dropping with its crystal and marble balusters. Equally so is a giant chandelier, said to be the largest in the world, which hangs from the

The last sultans

When Sultan Abdül Mecit was laying out the plans for Dolmabahçe, the Ottoman Empire was well into its last century. Its economy had been crumbling for some time, due to a *fatwah* on the printing press and other scientific advancements, waves of nationalist uprising throughout Ottoman lands and a string of disastrous military defeats to a new foe in the north: Tsarist Russia. Abdül Mecit's successor, Abdül Aziz, was more concerned with his harem of thousands than with matters of state. And the death knell of the sultans sounded when the last true autocrat, Abdül Hamid II, retreated within the walls of Yıldız Palace. In 1853 Tsar Nicholas I branded the Ottoman Empire the 'Sick Man of Europe'. The last sultan, Mehmet VI, was deposed in 1922 and left İstanbul quietly one night with his family on a train from Sirkeci Station, thus bringing to a close the reign of a dynasty that had lasted for almost five centuries.

Hayreddin Paşa statue

gilded ceiling of the immense **Throne Room**. The **Harem** is less ostentatious, but fascinating nonetheless. For all its Western architecture and lifestyle, it still has separate sections for the official wives and concubines, with a central meeting room for tea and embroidery.

BEŞIKTAŞ

To get to the port of **Beşiktaş**, another busy transport hub, head northeast along tree-lined Dolmabahçe Caddesi, which runs beside the outer walls of the palace and is adorned by a permanent exhibition of photographs chronicling the life of Mustafa Kemal Atatürk. Beşiktaş is a vibrant local neighbourhood set around a bus terminus, a series of ferry docks and a set of bustling streets, where you can buy everything from fresh fish to household goods, cheap clothes and pirated DVDs.

Naval Museum

The main point of tourist interest in the area is the **Naval Museum** ❸ (Deniz Müzesi; Hayrettin İskelesi Sokak; tel: 0212 327 4345; www.denizmuzeleri.tsk.tr; Wed–Sun 11am–5pm; charge), set on the western side of the waterside square and fronted by the trium-

Detail of Ottoman cannons on Beşiktaş' waterfront

Mustafa Kemal Atatürk

You may notice that all the clocks inside Dolmabahçe Palace are set to 9.05am. This was the time of death on 10 November 1938 of Mustafa Kemal Atatürk, founder of the Turkish Republic and its first president. The self-proclaimed 'Father of the Turks' is the country's most venerated modern leader. It is hard to pass a day in İstanbul without seeing an image of the man who liberated the country from occupying forces after World War I, before executing a series of modernising reforms. These included abolishing the sultanate and caliphate, moving the capital to Ankara and replacing Sharia (Islamic holy law) with civil, trade and penal codes adopted from the Swiss, French and Italians. Atatürk also gave women the vote, dropped the Ottoman script for the Latin alphabet and switched the fez hat for a European fedora.

Çırağan Palace Kempinski

Stag statue, Yıldız Park

phal statue of 16th-century Ottoman naval hero **Barbaros Hayreddin Paşa**. He is buried in a nearby **mausoleum** *(türbe)* in the northeastern corner of the square.

The museum will lure sailing enthusiasts with its displays of Ottoman naval paraphernalia, including antique maps and globes, navigation instruments and pistols. There's also an interesting assortment of artefacts from various naval engagements fought by the Turks over the centuries, such as the battle against the Venetians in the 16th century, the Dardanelles campaign of 1915 against the British and French, and the 1974 Cyprus conflict fought against the Greeks and Greek Cypriots.

Look out for the length of chain on display which used to be part of the impenetrable barrier that hung across the mouth of the Golden Horn in the days of the Byzantine Empire. The

story goes that, in order to surmount this blockade, Mehmet the Conqueror directed 70 of his ships to cross over into the estuary by land (using cows and hundreds of soldiers) from the Bosphorus, at the point where Dolmabahçe Palace now stands.

The gardens of the museum display a fascinating collection of caiques and Ottoman royal barges, as well as the remains of a German U-boat that sank in the Bosphorus during World War I.

Luxury hotels

From Besiktas, the road narrows as you walk along Çırağan Caddesi (the continuation of Dolmabahçe Caddesi). You will eventually pass two of the city's giant chain hotels on your right. The **Four Seasons Bosphorus 4** and the **Çırağan Palace Kempinski 5** have both been built upon the grounds of former Bosphorus palaces (see page 106). They are well worth a look inside or a stop for a cup of tea or cocktail on one of their luxurious outdoor terraces.

YILDIZ PARK

If you can blot out the noise of the traffic, try to imagine the route the sultans would have taken from the palace to their peaceful hunting retreat at Yildiz Park. Across the road from the main entrance to the Çırağan Palace Kempinski is the **Küçük Mecidiye Mosque 6** (Küçük Mecidiye Camii), built in 1843 for Sultan Abdül Mecit, which

Chalet Pavilion

marks the entrance to **Yıldız Park** (daily 9am–6pm, until 5.30pm in winter). Set on the slopes of a hill, Yıldız is one of İstanbul's prettiest parks and is very popular with weekend strollers. The city's parks are very popular in April when the tulips are in bloom, and in May when the lovely pink-blossomed Judas trees come into bloom.

In Yıldız you can find shady and peaceful respite from the city, while nursing a coffee in the gardens of its historic pavilions. It is quite a trek up to the pavilions; if you are not feeling up to it, continue your stroll to Ortaköy by going straight along Çırağan Caddesi.

Historic pavilions

Otherwise, head up the main path that leads into the park until near the top you have the choice of turning left towards the **Tent Pavilion** ❼ (Cadır Köşkü), which now serves as a café, or right towards the **Chalet Pavilion** ❽ (Şale Köşkü; Tue–Wed and Fri–Sun 9am–5pm; charge), located at the top of the park. This attractive residence was built by Abdül Hamid II in 1882 for his guests, but the paranoid sultan ended up moving there himself until he was deposed in 1909, living a solitary life as a carpenter amid the verdant gardens.

A short way to the southeast is the ornate **Malta Pavilion** (Malta Köşkü). Once a lodge used for resting during hunts, the building is now a café and restaurant, see ❶. Enter through the octagonal entrance hall, then walk downstairs past the fountain and onto the terrace overlooking the forest.

ORTAKÖY

Increasingly popular with day-tripping and nightclubbing locals, the once sleepy fishing village of **Ortaköy** ❾, 3km (2 miles) up the coast road from Dolmabahçe, is today a vibrant waterside community, with shops, restaurants and *nargile* cafés surrounding its stunning 19th-century mosque.

The fastest way to reach Ortaköy is via Palanga Caddesi, which can be accessed from a park gateway a few dozen metres down the hill from the Malta Pavilion. After descending to the main road, Muallim Naci Caddesi, cross over and head towards the pier down Vapur Iskelesi Sokak. This leads to **Ortaköy Square** (Ortaköy Meydanı), where the sea wall is lapped by the waves of the Bosphorus and fishing boats bob in the swell in front of the Büyük Mecidiye Mosque.

To your right, just before the pier, is a cluster of cafés and restaurants, which are a great lunch or dinner treat. They include the Asian-fusion restaurant **Banyan**, see ❷, and ever-popular **The House Café**, see ❸. More traditional eating options at the centre of the square come in the form of local *meyhanes* like **Çınaraltı**, see ❹. Stalls selling *kumpir* (jacket potatoes) and fruit-filled waffles offer a cheaper fill.

Büyük Mecidiye Mosque

Wade through the sea of pigeons to arrive at the **Büyük Mecidiye Mosque** ❿ (Büyük Mecidiye Camii), a neo-Baroque edifice built in 1856 by the same architects who designed the Dolmabahçe Palace and Dolmabahçe Mosque. In the afternoon sun, which casts light through the decorative grilles over the windows, it's a sublime sight. Look out for the large calligraphies produced by Sultan Abdül Mecit himself.

The backstreets behind Ortaköy Square are a pleasure to explore, especially on Sundays when the **flea market** is in full swing, and you can buy anything from jewellery and pashminas to leather handbags.

Heading back

Returning to Kabataş is easy: cabs are frequent on the main strip Muallim Naci Caddesi, and buses 22RE and 25E pass regularly from the stop next to the beginning of Taş Basamak Sokak.

Food and Drink

❶ MALTA KÖŞKÜ

Yıldız Parkı; tel: 0212 258 9453; daily 9am–10.30pm; $$

An elegant stop in the woods for refreshments or a light meal, with a view over the Bosphorus. There's a buffet for weekend brunches, and sandwiches and desserts for lunch and snacks. The dinner menu has a more Turkish influence.

❷ BANYAN

Salhane Sokak 3, Ortaköy; tel: 0212 259 9060; www.banyanrestaurant.com; Mon–Sat noon–2am; Sun 10am–2am; $$$

Reserve a table on the waterside terrace at this top-floor, top-notch Asian-fusion restaurant. Start with some sashimi or a mixed appetiser plate, then try the sea bass steamed in banana leaves or the sake-marinated chargrilled filet mignon.

❸ THE HOUSE CAFÉ

Salhane Sokak 1, Ortaköy; tel: 0212 227 2699; www.thehousecafe.com.tr; Mon–Thur and Sun 8am–1am, Fri–Sat 8am–2am; $$$

This hip joint with a waterfront terrace is one of a city-wide chain, serving burgers, pizzas and salads to İstanbul's bright young things, who flock here for jazzy cocktails and a laid-back atmosphere. No reservations taken so expect to wait.

❹ ÇINARALTI

İskele Meydanı 28, Ortaköy; tel: 0212 261 4616; www.cinaralti.com; daily noon–1am; $$

A traditional *meyhane* offering hot and cold *meze* and an extensive menu of fresh fish, prepared at your request.

Ottoman houses, Arnavutköy

BOSPHORUS VILLAGES

Take a memorable walk along the edge of the Bosphorus through five former fishing villages, enjoying spectacular views of the Asian shore from the heights of the Rumeli Fortress, or from the terrace of Muzedechanga, the Sakıp Sabancı Museum's superb gourmet restaurant.

DISTANCE: 6.75km (4 miles)
TIME: 5 hours
START: Les Ottomans hotel, Kuruçeşme
END: Sakıp Sabancı Museum, Emirgan
POINTS TO NOTE: This walk can be significantly shortened by almost 2km (over a mile) by catching a bus or taxi between Rumeli Hisarı and Emirgan. The waterside path is exposed to the elements, so try to pick a calm, rain-free day.

Just decades ago, the villages beside the Bosphorus north of Ortaköy were small, tranquil enclaves inhabited, as they had been for centuries, by fishermen who earned their livelihoods from the spoils of the strait. Today the villages have been subsumed within the expanding metropolis, while land along the Bosphorus has become coveted real estate.

Despite recent development, however, the Bosphorus shore has managed to maintain a sense of its former serenity; the sleepy streets of Arnavut-köy stand in stark contrast to the hubbub of Beyoğlu.

Coast Road

The unbroken stretch of road that runs from Kabataş all the way up to the Black Sea is known by locals as the **Sahil Yolu** (Coast Road). It is particularly suited for pedestrians on the stretch between Kuruçeşme and Rumeli Hisarı, where there is a walkway that skirts the sea for the whole distance.

KURUÇEŞME

Arrive at **Kuruçeşme ❶** by taxi, or take buses 22, 22RE or 25E from Kabataş, or 40, 40T or 42T from Taksim Square. A perfect way to start the tour is with a coffee at the opulent **Les Ottomans** (Muallim Naci Caddesi 168; tel: 0212 359 1500; www.lesottomans.com.tr), an Ottoman mansion that has been turned into an exclusive boutique hotel. The interior, put together by local design guru Zeynep Fadıloğlu, is a dazzling fusion of traditional Turkish motifs and contemporary styles.

Fishing boats   *Les Ottomans hotel*

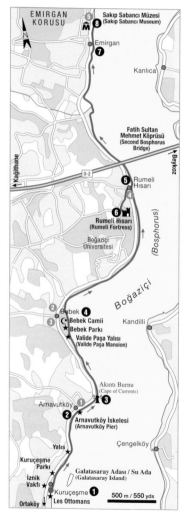

Kuruçeşme Park

Turn right out of Les Ottomans and head north, joining the Bosphorus towpath; it begins in **Kuruçeşme Park** (Kuruçeşme Parkı) and runs beside a line of moored boats, many of which are available for hire (see page 70). Peeping out of the Bosphorus to your right is the **Galatasaray Island** (Galatasaray Adası, also known as Su Ada), a leisure complex owned by Galatasaray Football Club. This hip, open-all-hours complex boasts two swimming pools and a host of restaurants, bars and clubs. It is particularly good for summertime swimming and lounging while hanging out with rich trendy İstanbullus. Shuttle boats leave regularly from Kuruçeşme Park.

Across the road to your left is the **İznik Tile Foundation** (İznik Vakfı; Öksüz Çocuk Sokak 7; tel: 0212 287 3243; www.iznik.com). Tourists and locals alike come here to peruse the selection of high-quality tiles and other ceramics. The foundation's workshops use production methods revived from Ottoman times. Designs include depictions of the region's fruit and olive trees, or ships, all extremely popular motifs. The toughest, highest quality (and priciest) tiles are not ceramic-based but made from locally quarried quartz. Quartz-rich tiles are porous to air, have excellent acoustic qualities (hence their use in mosques), and make good insulators as they contract slightly in winter and expand in summer.

Waterside Ottoman mansions

ARNAVUTKÖY

Founded by Albanian immigrants in the 15th century, **Arnavutköy** ❷, 'Albanian Village', is one of the most attractive villages on the Bosphorus due to its abundant *yalıs*. These wooden Ottoman mansions built by the water were once popular with the aristocracy, who followed the imperial court's move from Topkapı down to Dolmabahçe. You will see a group of them to the left as you head towards the centre of Arnatvutköy.

Take the road that forks left to the **village centre** just before the **Arnavutköy Pier** (Arnavutköy İskelesi). Here, fish restaurants and cafés line a shaded street sheltered from the breezes of the Bosphorus. You could stop for a fish lunch at any one (see also page 115); alternatively, try the excellent **Abracadabra**, see ❶. It is hard to miss, situated in a bright-burgundy four-storey yalı facing the main road and looking out over the water.

Cape of Currents

From here, cross the main road back over to the waterside path. There is a small white **lighthouse** on the promontory just after Arnavutköy, where the road curves round to Bebek. Named **Akıntı Burnu** ❸ (Cape of Currents), this is the point where the Bosphorus is at its deepest. Children often use the spot for bathing antics, jumping in the water and letting the strong (often dangerous) current take them upstream.

BEBEK

The next village along is **Bebek** ❹. One of the more affluent areas on the European shore, it is known for its chichi cafés and restaurants and the ladies who lunch therein. The first thing you will see as you approach is an impressive, but decaying, white yalı. The 1902 **Valide Paşa Mansion**

Bosphorus cruise

To see the Bosphorus villages in style, consider chartering one of the many yachts docked around Kuruçeşme or between Bebek and Rumeli Hisarı. The vessels range from small water taxis to wooden sailing boats and luxury cruisers; their prices vary accordingly. The captains are often on board, and are open to negotiations. Look to pay in the region of $500 for a four-hour trip, although if your party is small, haggle for all you are worth. Take your own food and drink, which will be served to you on deck, and go in the early evening to catch the sunset. Check out Istanbul Tours (tel: 0212 225 1967; www.toursistanbul. com) or if you really want to splash out in style, try www.adaturizm.com, which provides more luxurious one-day cruises. Cheaper, although no less cheerful, are Bosphorus Tours (tel: 0554 797 2646; www.bosphorustour.com).

Open kitchen at Abracadabra

Cruise vessels at Kuruçeşme

(Valide Paşa Yalısı) serves as the Egyptian Embassy and marks the entrance to **Bebek Park** (Bebek Parkı), site of a wooden pier and ferry dock, and a host of small wooden fishing boats and water taxis knocking against the sea wall.

At the northern end of the park is the **Bebek Mosque** (Bebek Camii), also known as the Humayun Uabad Camii, a relatively new building constructed in 1912 by Sultan Mehmet V, the penultimate Ottoman sultan.

Refreshment options

From here, head down Bebek's main street, **Cevdet Paşa Caddesi**. If you are thirsty, stop at one of the several chain cafés on the right-hand side. They might not look like much from the street, but their terraces literally hang over the Bosphorus and make an exhilarating setting for a humble cuppa.

Another great view can be had at **Mangerie**, see ❷, a third-floor-terrace café a little further down the main street on the left-hand side.

For deli delicacies, try **Meşur Bebek Badem Ezmesi** (Cevdet Paşa Caddesi 53C; tel: 0212 263 5984) which has been selling delicious marzipan bars for over a century, or **Taylieli Olive Oil** (at 46D; tel: 0212 265 6617) whose eco-friendly bottled product is distributed worldwide.

Alternatively, if you are looking for something with local flavour and a little easier on the pocket, head back along the street for **Bebek Köftecisi**, see ❸, an unassuming café opposite the park, which serves up mouth-watering meatballs and barbecued chicken thighs.

RUMELİ HİSARI

A 1.5km (1-mile) stretch of apartment buildings and moored motorboats separate Bebek from the next village, **Rumeli Hisarı** ❺. Named after the monumental military castle perched on the hill above the main road, the neighbourhood has a noticeably more relaxed and bohemian feel than its predecessor, with a line of outdoor cafés and eateries running between the castle entrance and the immense shadow of the **Second Bosphorus Bridge**. Named the Fatih Sultan Mehmet Bridge (Fatih Sultan Mehmet Köprüsü) after the Ottoman conqueror, this engineering giant is currently the 14th-largest bridge of its kind in the world.

One of the Bosphorus's most famous fish restaurants, **İskele**, is also here, occupying the building of the former village pier, see ❹.

Rumeli fortress

The **fortress** ❻ (Rumeli Hisarı Müzesi; Thur–Tue 9.30am–4pm; charge) was hastily built by Sultan Mehmet II in the run-up to his invasion of Constantinople in 1452. It is said that so great was his urgency to secure its construction, the sultan carried bricks and stones

The Bosphorus from Rumeli Hisarı

with his own hands. Rumeli Hisarı went up in a barely conceivable four and a half months.

Located at the narrowest point of the Bosphorus strait (660m/2,165ft), the fortification mirrors Anadolu Hisarı (see page 93) on the Asian shore, which was put up by Beyazıt I in 1393. The two castles – poised on either side of the strait's natural bottleneck – enabled the Turks greater control over ships passing to and from the Black Sea.

Climbing up the walls

Composed of three main towers and a huge defensive wall that encircles a valley, the fortress affords some terrific views of this part of the city. Although there is not much to see within the confines of the walls – a lonely minaret and a small, functioning amphitheatre sit in the centre among the foliage – the real fun of visiting the structure lies in clambering around the ramparts and climbing the steps to the dizzying heights of the towers, which stretch up to 28m (90ft) high. Vertigo sufferers beware!

EMIRGAN

From Rumeli Hisarı, it's a 20-minute walk to the next attractive point on the Bosphorus, **Emirgan** ❼. As the road here leaves the water's edge, you might wish to consider jumping in a cab or hailing a 25E or 22RE bus to speed your journey.

Sakıp Sabancı Museum

The main draw of Emirgan is the stately **Sakıp Sabancı Museum** ❽ (Sakıp Sabancı Müzesi; Sakıp Sabancı Caddesi 42; tel: 0212 277 2200; http://muze. sabanciuniv.edu; Tue, Thur–Sun 10am–6pm, Wed 10am–10pm; charge). Its bucolic setting – located within an immaculately manicured garden on a hill over a peaceful village square beneath – perhaps belies the fact that this 1927 mansion is the former home of one of Turkey's leading industrial families.

The museum houses Sakıp Sabancı's impressive collection of paintings and calligraphies, as well as a far more popular wing that hosts a programme of international art shows. In recent years there have been retrospectives of Picasso, Rodin and Salvador Dalí.

Fortress entrance

Rumeli Fortress

While you are here, check out the café-restaurant **Muzedechanga**, see ❺, which was recently voted best new restaurant by a leading global design magazine. Serving an all-day menu, it becomes smarter in the evening.

Heading back
Retrace your steps a little way along Sakıp Sabancı Caddesi to catch the 22, 22RE or 25E buses back to Kabataş, or the 40, 40T or 42T buses back to Taksim Square.

Food and Drink

❶ ABRACADABRA
Arnavutköy Caddesi 50/1; tel: 0212 358 6087; www.abracadabra-ist.com; Tue–Thur 10am–midnight, Fri–Sun 10am–2am; $$
Chef and restaurateur Dilara Erbay has set up an easy-going and homely restaurant over four floors of a converted Ottoman *yalı*. Erbay oversees the open kitchen, which offers original cooking with a Turkish twist. Look out for the garlic snails and the salmon *çiğ köfte*, delicious balls of spiced raw fish.

❷ MANGERIE
Cevdet Paşa Caddesi 69, Bebek; tel: 0212 263 5199; www.mangeriebebek.com; daily 8am–midnight; $$$
A trendy Bebek institution, Mangerie has whitewashed wooden walls and cosy sofas looking out over the Bosphorus to the Asian shore. Sandwiches and burgers are a good lunch staple here, and the salads are excellent.

❸ BEBEK KÖFTECISI
Hamam Sokak 4, Bebek; 0212 263 6361; Mon–Sat 8am–9pm; $
For tasty local fare that won't break the bank, head up the steps of Hamam Sokak to this modest grill joint. There's a daily special soup and main course, as well as a permanent menu of meats fresh off the barbecue. The chicken thighs (*piliç but*) are highly recommended.

❹ ISKELE
Yahya Kemal Caddesi 1, Rumeli Hisarı; tel: 0212 263 2997; www.rumelihisariiskele.com; daily noon–midnight; $$$
Fish, fish and more fish are served at this well-heeled restaurant set inside Rumeli Hisarı's wooden pier building. Start with some *meze*, and ask your waiter about the day's specials.

❺ MUZEDECHANGA
Sakıp Sabancı Caddesi 42, Emirgan; 0212 323 0901; www.changa-istanbul.com; Tue–Sun 10.30am–1am; $$$
A spacious interior, huge outdoor terrace and delicious international menu make for a museum restaurant that's a cut above the average. Try the fennel with fava beans, spicy Turkish sausage (*sucuk*) or spinach and cheese tortellini.

Beyazıt Mosque

THE IMPERIAL MOSQUES

Venture back in time to the 15th and 16th centuries, the golden era of the Ottoman Empire, by visiting the imperial mosques of Beyazıt, Süleymaniye and Fatih, looking out for the ancient Valens Aqueduct on the way.

DISTANCE: 4.75km (3 miles)
TIME: A leisurely day
START: Old Book Bazaar
END: Saray Muhallebicisi, Fatih
POINTS TO NOTE: In order to see the market at Fatih, you should plan to go on a Wednesday. Female visitors should not forget their long sleeves, long trousers and headscarves for this mosque-abundant tour.

West of the Grand Bazaar, the neighbourhoods of Beyazıt, Süleymaniye and Fatih are often overlooked by tourists. But this is to miss out on the city's two largest mosque complexes, at Fatih and Süleymaniye. Their *medreses*, *hamams*, *türbes* (tombs) and *imarets* (kitchens) remain a testament to life at the height of the empire.

BEYAZIT

Mehmet the Conqueror, who took the city from the Roman Byzantines in 1453, constructed his first palace at **Beyazıt**, adjacent to the ancient Forum of Theodosius, which was traditionally considered the city centre.

Old Book Bazaar

Set off from the **Old Book Bazaar ❶** (Sahaflar Çarşısı), situated between Beyazıt Mosque and Çadırcılar Caddesi, which runs beside the Grand Bazaar. This little courtyard serves both the university and mosque with its new and second-hand books, from academic textbooks to Arabic Qu'rans. Other shops, such as **Ottoman Miniatures** at stall no. 18, sell Ottoman miniature paintings and antiquarian maps.

Beyazıt Mosque

Pass through the bazaar to **Beyazıt Square** (Beyazıt Meydanı), which stands on the site of the Forum of Theodosius, and enter the mosque via the courtyard to your left. **Beyazıt Mosque ❷** (Beyazıt Camii) was built in 1506 by the austere and pious Sultan Beyazıt II, son of Mehmet the Conqueror, and is the oldest surviving imperial mosque in İstanbul.

İstanbul University   *Copy of the Qur'an in Turkish and Arabic*

The subtle, symmetrical design of the mosque marks the beginning of a distinctive Ottoman architectural style: note the resemblance of the structure to Hagia Sophia.

İstanbul University

The giant Moorish gateway on the northern side of Beyazıt Square is the entrance to **İstanbul University** ❸ (İstanbul Üniversitesi), which houses in its grounds the **Beyazıt Tower** (Beyazıt Kulesi), an 85m (279ft) -high stone structure, which was erected in 1828 as a lookout point for fires.

The university itself, founded at the time of the Ottoman Conquest, is the largest public university in Turkey, with

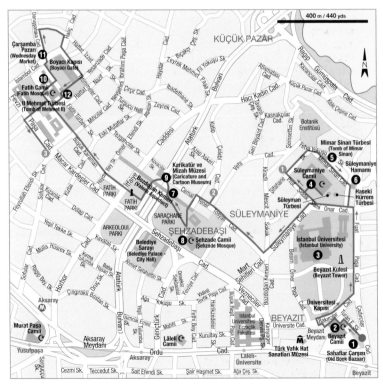

Süleymaniye Mosque

around 60,000 registered students. It has been the site of many student demonstrations over the years, including the bloody clashes between students and police in 1960 that preceded the 27 May coup d'état and deposition of Prime Minister Adnan Menderes.

Entrance to the campus (but not Beyazıt Tower, which is closed) is usually permitted to non-students, if you show a passport at the main gates. You can also catch a glimpse of the tower through the gates on Fuat Paşa Caddesi, along the eastern side of the university walls, which you can reach by turning right and taking the next left.

Mimar Sinan

Undoubtedly the greatest classical Ottoman architect, Koca Mimar (meaning architect) Sinan was responsible for some of the most impressive structures of the empire's history, including Süleymaniye Mosque, Şehzade Mosque (see page 78), Caferağa Medresesi in Sultanahmet (see page 43) and Rüstem Paşa Mosque in Eminönü (see page 50). Appointed Imperial Architect by Süleyman in 1538, Sinan's career went on to span another 50 years, during which time he constructed a jaw-dropping 321 buildings, 85 of which are still intact in İstanbul. His hallmark majestic domes, and his innovative use of space and light, have earned him comparisons with his Italian contemporary Michelangelo.

SÜLEYMANIYE MOSQUE

Follow Fuat Paşa Caddesi, then turn left into Prof. Sıddık Sami Onar Caddesi, which leads to the entrance to the gardens around **Süleymaniye Mosque** ❹ (Süleymaniye Camii; daily 9am–5pm; free). The mosque complex (*külliye*), completed in 1557, is considered the masterwork of the great Ottoman architect, Mimar Sinan (see box), and a lasting testimony to the empire's longest-ruling sultan, Süleyman I, also known as Süleyman the Magnificent.

Great-grandson of Mehmet the Conqueror, Süleyman reigned from 1520 to 1566, during which time the Ottoman Empire doubled the span of its territory. With the spoils of war and a large percentage of taxes coming back to the sultan, the palace coffers were overflowing with funds ready to build a lasting testament to his power and glory.

Inside the Mosque

The mosque's main dome stands a staggering 47m (156ft) above a prayer hall of more than 3,300 sq m (35,500 sq ft) in area. The tile work and stained glass of the prayer hall are exquisite; the calligraphy on the inside of the domes was executed by one of the finest artists of the period, Ahmet Karahısarı. Flanking the mosque are four minarets traditionally held to represent Süleyman's status as the fourth sultan in the city.

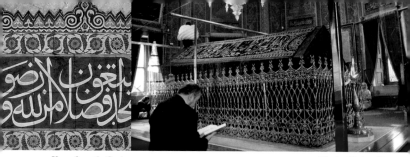

Verses from the Qur'an   *Tomb of Sultan Fatih*

Surrounding the main entrance of the mosque is a porticoed courtyard; its 24 columns are thought to have been salvaged from the Byzantine royal box at the Hippodrome. The quiet gardens of the larger enclosure surrounding the mosque are a perfect place to unwind, with a panoramic view of the Golden Horn.

On the southeastern side of the garden complex are the **Tomb of Süleyman** (Süleyman Türbesi) and adjacent **Tomb of Roxelana** (Haseki Hürrem Türbesi). Brought to Istanbul as a slave girl from Russia, Roxelana rose through the ranks to become the sultan's favourite. Süleyman's octagonal mausoleum contains twice as many tiles as there are inside the mosque, and is shared by his daughter Mihrimah, and sultans Ahmet II and Süleyman II.

Refreshment options

Leave the garden courtyard by the same way you entered, and turn right on Prof. Sıddık Sami Onar Caddesi. This part of the street was once known as 'Addicts Alley' from the days when its cafés were notorious for their supply of recreational drugs. Today, they sell tea, coffee and light refreshments, although much more enticing is the **Lale Bahçesi**, see ①, just around the corner on Şifahane Sokak. If you are in need of a more substantial lunch, head next door to **Dârüzziyafe**, see page 116, set in a former mosque kitchen building that used to provide food for the poor.

Mimar Sinan's Tomb

Continue up Şifahane Sokak to the corner with Mimar Sinan Caddesi, which is the site of the **Tomb of Mimar Sinan ⑤** (Mimar Sinan Türbesi), a humble structure he designed himself.

Süleymaniye Hamam

Further down at the end of the same street is the **Süleymaniye Hamam ⑥** (see page 23), which was part of the original mosque complex. Restored to working order, it is one of the few hamams in the city centre that allows for mixed-gender bathing.

From here leave the Süleymaniye complex by way of Prof. Sıddık Sami Onar Caddesi, turning left into Süleymaniye Caddesi, which is likely to be thronged with students from the university during term-time.

VALENS AQUEDUCT

After 250m/yds, cross the junction and head northwest along Cemal Yener Tosyalı Caddesi, where, after 400m/yds, you could make a quick right on Katip Çelebi Caddesi for a cup of *boza* at the **Vefa Bozacısı**, see ②. A thick, gooey cream-coloured drink, *boza* is made from fermented bulgur, water and sugar, and reputedly infused with a cocktail of vitamins.

Look to your left to see the remains of the two-storey **Valens Aqueduct ⑦** (Bozdoğan Kemeri). Completed in the 4th century by Emperor Valens,

Valens Aqueduct

this particular length of the conduit connected the third and fourth hills of Constantinople, and was part of a complicated system of water transport and distribution, comprising more than 250km (155 miles) of waterways. It was still in use until the end of the 19th century, having been reinforced with iron piping by the Ottomans.

Şehzade Mosque

Turn left into Akıf Paşa Sokak and pass under the aqueduct arch into **Sara-çhane Park**, a garden at the edge of **Şehzade Mosque ❽** (Şehzade Camii). Süleyman the Magnificent commissioned this complex in memory of his first son, Mehmet, who died from smallpox at the age of 21; it was completed in 1548 by Sinan. For an imperial mosque, Şehzade (meaning 'prince') has an austere interior, with no columns or balconies to break the empty space.

Caricature and Cartoon Museum

Walk northwest out of the park and cross over the hectic **Atatürk Bulvarı**, passing back under the aqueduct arches blackened with exhaust fumes. Head for the little *medrese* building set against the northern side of the aqueduct. It is now the **Caricature and Cartoon Museum ❾** (Karikatür ve Mizah Müzesi; Kovacilar Sokak 12; tel: 0212 521 12 64; Tue–Sat 9am–5pm; free), exhibiting Turkish cartoons and humorous drawings from the beginning of the 20th century. Every year the museum displays the entries for the Nasreddin Hoca competition, a selection of comical drawings of the Turkish humourist who has become an emblem for irreverent comedy and irony in the country.

FATIH

Go back through the arches, cross **Fatih Park** to join with Büyük Karaman Caddesi, and walk northwest for 450m/yds in the direction of the Fatih Mosque.

There are no visible bars or nightclubs in this conservative area, where Islamist politicians and radical religious groups have the strongest foothold. Here, life revolves around the mosque and the Islamic clothes stores (and dessert shops) on the main Fevzi Paşa Caddesi. Veiled women covered from head to toe by their black *abayas* are a much more common sight here than anywhere else in İstanbul.

Having taken Constantinople in 1453, the conqueror *(fatih)*, Mehmet II, commissioned **Fatih Mosque ❿** (Fatih Camii). Completed in 1471, it is the largest complex to be constructed in the Ottoman Empire, rebuilt by Mehmet III in 1771 after the original building was completely destroyed by an earthquake five years before.

Wednesday Market

Exit the complex via the **Boyacı Gate** (Boyacı Kapısı) on the northwestern side. Here, on Wednesdays, a teeming

Fatih Mosque ceiling   *Muslim woman in Fatih*

market stretches through the streets in every direction. The **Wednesday Market** ⑪ (Çarşamba Pazarı) sees veiled women come out in droves to buy tomatoes, spinach and rice, inspect the rolling pins and wooden spoons, and barter for clothing, shoes or bags of wool.

Walk straight down Daruşşafaka Caddesi, past the sumptuous fruit-and-vegetable stalls, and make a U-turn by taking a right and then another to bring you back to Tetimmeler Caddesi, where the shoes and clothing stalls begin. Here too are the outer walls of the mosque complex, which you can re-enter by turning right into Yesarizade Caddesi.

Follow the path around to the left of the mosque and pass though the stone doorway that leads to the cemetery and **Tomb of Mehmet II** ⑫ (II Mehmet Türb-

esi). This octagonal marble building, with its flamboyant portico, is the resting place of the great conqueror. It was ceremoniously visited by each of his successors on the day of coronation.

Fevzi Paşa Caddesi

Now head down towards Fatih's main thoroughfare, **Fevzi Paşa Caddesi**, by way of the steps on the southwestern side of the courtyard, and lose yourself among the evening shoppers milling around the boutiques and the multitude of wedding-dress shops. You could end your day with a sweet treat or a grilled kebab at the **Saray Muhallebicisi**, see ③, before hailing a cab or catching a bus back; the 28, 31E, 32, 36KE, 37E, 38E and 90 all go to Eminönü, while the 87 will take you to Taksim Square (Taksim Meydani).

Food and Drink

① LALE BAHÇESİ
Şifahane Sokak 12, Süleymaniye; tel: 0212 512 7882; L and AT; $
A simple café set in a picturesque sunken garden, which has a large fire in its courtyard during the colder months. Serves refreshments and some basic food.

② VEFA BOZACISI
Katip Çelebi Caddesi 104/1, Vefa; tel: 0212 519 4922; www.vefa.com.tr; daily 8am– midnight; $

This establishment was once frequented by Atatürk himself (his cup is kept on display), and prides itself on the strength of its main product, the fermented bulgur drink *boza*.

③ SARAY MUHALLEBICISI
Fevzi Paşa Caddesi 1, Fatih; tel: 0212 521 0505; www.saraymuhallebicisi.com; daily 6am–1am; $
This long-established chain of Turkish canteen-style restaurants specialises in mouth-watering desserts. Try their *tavuk göğsü*, a sweet made from finely chopped chicken breast.

Virgin Mary and Child fresco

OLD CITY WALLS

Travel to the outer limits of Old Constantinople to visit the colossal Theodosian Walls, see the gate where Mehmet the Conqueror entered the city for the first time, then head over to the Kariye Museum to view İstanbul's most impressive Byzantine mosaics and frescoes.

DISTANCE: 2.5km (1.5 miles)
TIME: 3 hours
START: Edirne Gate
END: Ayvansaray Caddesi
POINTS TO NOTE: There are regular buses to Edirne Gate from Eminönü (31E, 32, 37E and 38E), from Beyazıt by the edge of the Grand Bazaar (36E, 38, 39 and 39Ç) or from Taksim Square (87 and 77MT). This tour could be combined with either a visit to Fener and Balat (route 12) or Eyüp (route 13), both a short bus ride away from the end point.

The walls of Constantinople run in fits and starts from Ayvansaray on the Golden Horn right down to Yedikule on the Sea of Marmara. They were built in the 5th century during the reign of Emperor Theodosius II, and what remains of them is still an impressive sight, as are the ruins of the Palace of the Sovereign. While walking the entire 6.5km (4 miles) of the wall is tiring and at times uneventful, the area from the

Edirne Gate up to the Golden Horn is well worth exploring, especially because of the nearby Kariye Museum.

EDIRNE GATE

One of eight main entrances, the **Edirne Gate ❶** (Edirnekapı) was where Sultan Mehmet II stormed into Constantinople in 1452. Today the original gate is marked with a commemorative plaque, just off Kaleboyu Caddesi. Next to the gate is the **Mihrimah Sultan Mosque** (Mihrimah Sultan Camii), built by Sinan in 1565 for Süleyman's favourite daughter.

KARIYE MUSEUM

Walk past the mosque, cross busy Fevzi Paşa Caddesi and head down Şeyh Eyüp Sokak, following signs to **Kariye Museum ❷** (Kariye Müzesi, within the Kariye Mosque; tel: 0212 631 9241; www.chora museum.com; Thur–Tue mid-Apr–1 Oct 9am–6pm, winter 9am–4.30pm, times subject to change; charge). If you get lost in the winding streets, ask any local for

Kariye Museum   *The Anastasis fresco*

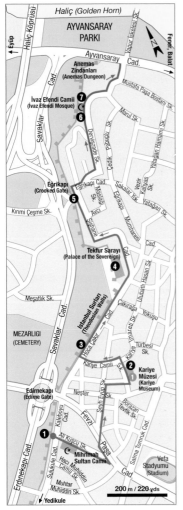

'Kareeyeh'. The jewel in İstanbul's Byzantine crown, the former church of St Saviour in Chora was restored and opened as a museum in 1958.

The oldest part of the building, the central domed area, dates back to 1120. Rebuilt and decorated in the 14th century, the church was converted into a mosque in 1511; fortunately, it was not substantially altered and the artwork was covered with wooden screens.

Mosaics and frescoes

The now uncovered and spectacularly preserved mosaics and frescoes, dating from between 1310 and 1320 (probably the work of a single unknown artist), are grouped into four narrative cycles depicting the lives of Christ and the Virgin Mary, along with portraits of saints.

Each tiny tile is set at a different angle to its neighbours, so that the reflected light creates the illusion of a shimmering, ethereal image. The frescoes are all in the parecclesion, which stretches the length of the building and was used in Byzantine times as a funerary chapel. The artist's masterpiece is the *Anastasis* (Resurrection) in the vault of the apse, showing Christ pulling Adam and Eve from their tombs, while Satan lies bound beneath his feet.

Next door is the Kariye Hotel and its restaurant, **Asitane**, see ❶. a great spot for lunch. For something more modest, choose from one of the cafés on the courtyard in front of the museum.

Theodosian Walls

THEODOSIAN WALLS

On leaving the museum, head west along Kariye Camii Sokak towards the 5th-century **Theodosian Walls ❸** (İstanbul Surları), which you can follow all the way to the Golden Horn. You can climb a portion of them via the **steps**, a few metres after taking a right onto Hoca Çakır Caddesi. It's a short, steep climb, rewarded by spectacular views. Be careful – there is no guardrail up here.

The land walls were 5m (16ft) thick and towered 12m (40ft) above the city, guarded by 96 towers. The Byzantines built magnificent houses and palaces along the walls, which have sadly all but disappeared. For around 800 years the walls kept out invaders, until breached by the crusaders in 1204 and by the Ottoman Turks 250 years later.

Remains of Byzantine palaces

Continue downhill and you will pass a brick façade with an upper row of arches that once belonged to the **Palace of the Sovereign ❹** (Tekfur Sarayı), erected between the 13th and 14th centuries and probably an extension of Blachernae Palace. After the conquest it became a zoo where the sultans kept exotic animals given as gifts; today the area is called Ayvansaray (animal castle).

After the palace, turn left and follow Şişhane Caddesi, which ends up at **Eğrikapı ❺** (Crooked Gate). The gate takes its name from the narrow lane that enters the city through the gate and skirts around a mausoleum.

From the gate, turn left as the road forks and take the second left, Dervişzade Sokak, downhill to the late 16th-century **İvaz Efendi Mosque ❻** (İvaz Efendi Camii), where the **Blachernae Palace** once stood (only traces remain). If the mosque is open, look inside – although tiny, it is said to be the work of Sinan and contains lovely İznik tiles.

Behind the mosque is the **Anemas Dungeon ❼** (Anemas Zindanları; closed for restoration), where deposed emperors were imprisoned and tortured.

Continue downhill until Dervişzade Sokak meets the coast road, Ayvansaray Caddesi. From here, buses go west to Eyüp (see route 13), or east to Fener, Balat and Eminönü (see routes 5 and 12).

Sunday mass at the Church of St George

FENER AND BALAT

Modern development has barely touched these maze-like Greek and Jewish quarters, which are perfect for a quiet stroll. Hidden away in this humble corner of the city is the headquarters of the Greek Orthodox Church.

DISTANCE: 2km (1.25 miles)
TIME: 3 hours
START: Fener bus stop
END: Eski Kasaplar Sokak, Balat
POINTS TO NOTE: Buses 399B and C from Eminönü and the 55T from Taksim run to the Fener bus stop.

Tucked into the southern side of the Golden Horn, not far from the limits of the old city walls, are the peaceful districts of Fener and Balat with their carless hilly streets.

FENER

Now fallen into decay, Fener was once a flourishing Greek neighbourhood. The families that lived here amassed huge fortunes from maritime trade and wielded considerable influence in the Ottoman Empire's foreign affairs.

From the Fener bus stop, walk to the **Greek Patriarchate ❶** (Rum Ortodoks Patrikhanesi; Dr Sadık Ahmet Caddesi), the spiritual centre of the world's 200

million Orthodox Christians, which has stood on this site since 1601. The only visitable part is the **Church of St George** (Aya Yorgi Kilisesi), dating back to 1720, where the collection of relics includes those of saint Gregory the Theologian.

If hungry, head back to the main road to eat at **Tarihi Haliç İşkembecisi**, see page 117, or **Fener Köşkü**, see ❶. Otherwise, take Yıldırım Caddesi northwest and then the third left to Vodina Caddesi, where **Kemha** at no. 6 sells interesting antiques. Turn left on Sancaktar Yokuşu and then right up the steps on Tekvii Merdivenli Sokak.

Two Churches

The red-brick, castle-like building dominating the Fener skyline is the 19th-century **Greek Secondary School ❷** (Özel Fener Rum Lisesi). Beside it in a walled-in complex is the **Church of St Mary of the Mongols ❸** (Kanlı Kilise). This fascinating 13th-century church is only occasionally open on Sundays, but try knocking on the door to see if the janitor is in to give you a tour (for a small fee). Many of the icons are blackened

Balat neighbourhood

from years of candle soot, although some, including a thousand-year-old Virgin Mary, can still be made out. A tiny staircase leads down to a tunnel, alleged to stretch to Hagia Sophia.

Turn left from the church, then take the second right to Kiremit Caddesi. Head north towards the Golden Horn, walking via Fener Külhanı Sokak, Vodina Caddesi and Yıldırım Caddesi, until you reach Mürsel Paşa Caddesi. A right turn here will bring you to **St Stephen of the Bulgars** ❹ (Sveti Stefan Kilisesi), made entirely from cast iron. It still serves İstanbul's tiny Bulgarian community.

BALAT

Balat was one of the city's main Jewish communities, swelling at the end of the 15th century with the expulsion of Jews from Spain. Welcomed by Sultan Beyazıt II, they became influential diplomats and merchants. Although numbers have since dwindled, Jews still live in Balat, home to several synagogues. The oldest is the **Ahrida Synagogue** ❺ on Kürkçü Çeşmesi Sokak. A short way north, narrow **Eski Kasaplar Sokak** ❻ gives a traditional flavour of the area. Catch a bus back to Eminönü from Mürsel Paşa Caddesi.

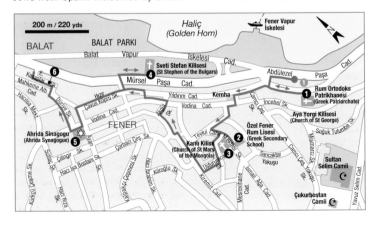

Eyüp Mosque

EYÜP

Make your way up the Golden Horn beyond the old city walls to the district of Eyüp, one of the most important centres of pilgrimage in the Islamic world. Discover the burial place of Eyüp Al-Ansari and marvel at the view from the Pierre Loti Teahouse.

DISTANCE: 1km (0.75 mile)
TIME: 2–3 hours
START: Eyüp Pier
END: Pierre Loti Teahouse
POINTS TO NOTE: Buses 399B, C or D run to Eyüp Pier from Eminönü. The 55T from Taksim Square stops a short walk away. Hourly ferries sail here from Üsküdar, Karaköy and Eminönü. The tombs open Tue–Sun until 4.30pm. This walk could be combined with a visit to the nearby city walls (route 11) or Fener and Balat (route 12).

Eyüp is one of İstanbul's holiest places and as a result has a devout, conservative feel. (You will probably feel more comfortable wearing longer sleeves and trousers/skirts. Women should carry a scarf to cover their hair when entering holy places.) The stunning mosque complex at its centre contains extensive cemetery grounds that house the tombs of Ottoman gentry, as well as Eyüp Al-Ansari, the Prophet Mohammed's standard bearer, who was killed during the first Arab siege of Constantinople in 674–8AD.

Located near the source of the Golden Horn, it's easy to get to Eyüp by taxi, bus or ferry from Eminönü, or by fishing boat from the Galata Bridge.

Eyüp can get crowded with local visitors during the weekend, as well as on a Friday, the main day of worship. At these times it's not unusual to see intense displays of emotion by devotees outside Eyüp Al-Ansari's tomb. Visit on a Sunday, and you are likely to see young boys lavishly dressed in white suits, fur-lined capes and plumed hats, visiting the mosque prior to the ritual ceremony of their *sünnet* (circumcision).

SOKULLU MEHMET PAŞA'S TOMB

Start at **Eyüp Pier** (Eyüp İskelesi) and walk along Eyüp İskele Sokak into Camii Kebir Sokak, a street lined with stalls selling religious souvenirs, prayer beads and Qur'ans. At the top of the street on the left is the **Tomb of the Grand Vizier Sokullu Mehmet Paşa** ❶ (Sokullu Mehmet Paşa Türbesi), designed by

Decorative interior, Eyüp Mosque

Sinan, who also built a mosque for the grand vizier (see page 37).

EYÜP MOSQUE

Just beyond the Tomb of Mehmet Paşa is a fountain at the centre of the square of **Eyüp Mosque** ❷ (Eyüp Camii). The mosque was originally commissioned by Mehmet the Conqueror in 1458, after a revelatory dream experienced by his *şeyhülislam* (religious governor) divulged the location of Eyüp Al-Ansari's tomb at the site of what was then called Cosmidion. Mehmet II's mosque was later rebuilt by Sultan Selim III in 1798.

Enter through the mosque's Baroque doorway into the first courtyard. Ladies who wish to enter should go through one of the doors immediately to the left and the right that lead to the women's section upstairs.

Tomb of Eyüp Al-Ansari

A doorway behind the *şadırvan* (the circular ablutions fountain) leads to the second courtyard and the **Tomb of Eyüp Al-Ansari** ❸ (Eyüp Sultan Türbesi). This mausoleum, with its intricately tiled exterior, is considered on a par with Damascus and Kerbala as a place of holy pilgrimage for Muslims,

and it's open to worshippers and tourists alike. The tomb also served as the site of a special coronation ceremony of new sultans, every one of whom from Mehmet the Conqueror onwards was girded here with the sword of the Osman, the first Ottoman patriarch.

MIHRIŞAH VALIDE SULTAN'S TOMB

Walk straight through the second courtyard to the back gateway and pass into the peaceful Sultan Reşat Caddesi to enter the **Tomb of Mihrişah Valide Sultan** ❹ (Mihrişah Valide Sultan Türbesi), mother of Selim II, who died in 1805. Next to the tomb is a *külliye* (mosque complex) built in 1794, which includes

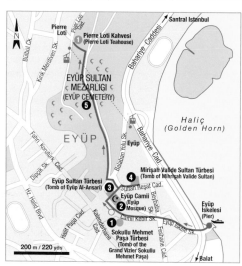

Eyüp cemetery

Pierre Loti Teahouse

a *mektep* (primary school) and an *imaret* (public kitchen).

Those of a more sensitive constitution might not want to stray into the area directly behind the complex, which is the site of the **Kurban Kesim Yeri**, the slaughterhouse for the sheep and goats. Animals are brought here in wheelbarrows to be given for religious sacrifice, after which a large amount of the meat is donated to the poor. Photography is not permitted in this area.

EYÜP CEMETERY

Retrace your steps along Sultan Reşat Caddesi to the end of the street and turn left along Balaban Yolu Sokak.

> ## Santralistanbul
>
> Another 2.5km (1.5 miles) up the Golden Horn, at the very last point of the estuary, is Santralistanbul (Kazım Karabekir Caddesi 1; tel: 0212 311 7878; www.santralistanbul.org; Mon–Fri 10am–6pm, Sat–Sun until 8pm; charge), a 19th-century Ottoman power station. Renovated by Bilgi University, the building is part of the university campus, but also functions as a superb museum (climb to the top of the building and check out the antiquated switches and dials in the former control room – great for kids) and a huge venue for contemporary art shows. To get there, catch a taxi or take the free shuttle bus that runs from Kabatas.

From here you can see a small path leading up the hill into the main **cemetery** ❺ on the right-hand side. You can climb to the top of the hill from here (it is a moderate 15-minute ascent), or you can walk the other way on Balaban Yolu Sokak and take the **cable car** (small charge) up to the Pierre Loti Teahouse.

Pierre Loti Teahouse

At the top of the hill, there are a small number of low-key establishments where visitors can sit and have a cup of tea inside or outdoors while gazing at the magnificent view. The **Pierre Loti Teahouse** (Pierre Loti Kahvesi), see ❶, is named after its most famous customer, a French naval officer and romantic writer called Pierre Loti (1850–1923), whose books lamented the growing Europeanisation of İstanbul. His most famous book, *Aziyadé*, chronicled a love affair with a Turkish girl of the same name whom he met on a trip to İstanbul in 1876.

Waterfront at Üsküdar

ÜSKÜDAR

Escape the tour groups of Sultanahmet and take a ferry across the Bosphorus to the Asian shore. Explore the fascinating mosques of Üsküdar before heading for a seaside stroll to the Maiden's Tower.

DISTANCE: 3.5km (2.25 miles) from Eminönü to Üsküdar; walking route: 2.25km (1.5 miles)

TIME: A half day

START: Üsküdar Pier

END: Maiden's Tower

POINTS TO NOTE: Ferries run every 20 minutes to Üsküdar from Eminönü (the first leaves 6.35am, the last returns 10.30pm) and Beşiktaş (the first leaves 7am, the last returns 9pm).

There has been a settlement at Üsküdar since around 686BC, making it more ancient than Byzantium on the European shore. It became popular with Ottoman philanthropists, who found the quiet neighbourhood ideal for building mosques and charitable institutions.

ÜSKÜDAR'S MOSQUES

Disembark from your ferry at **Üsküdar Pier** (Üsküdar İskelesi), cross the road and head towards the **Mihrimah Sultan**

Mosque ❶ (Mihrimah Sultan Camii), also known as the İskele (Pier) Camii. Built by Mimar Sinan in 1548 for Sultan Süleyman's daughter Mirimah, the mosque is defined by its double porch, which covers an attractive fountain.

Leave the mosque courtyard by the southern doorway, and look to the left for a calendar sundial with inscriptions in old Ottoman script attached to the wall. Make your way down Selmanağa Çeşme Sokak, passing on your right the elevator up to **Trend216**, see page 117, a good breakfast, brunch or lunch option. Cross the road, turn left and take the second right into Atlas Sokak, where there's a small **food market** specialising in fish and offal.

Exit into Hakimiyeti Milliye Caddesi and ahead you will see the **Mimar Sinan Çarşısı** ❷, an old *hamam* converted into a shopping arcade. Unless you have a fancy for footwear (shoe shops dominate here), continue to the building behind the arcade, the **Kara Davut Paşa Mosque** ❸ (Kara Davut Paşa Camii). This tiny structure has a unique three-domed design.

Mihrimah Sultan Mosque

Maiden's Tower

Yeni Valide Mosque

Turn back down the main street and take a left into the first doorway of the **Yeni Valide Mosque** ❹ (Yeni Valide Camii). Dodging the stray cats, walk around the courtyard and cemetery to the entrance at the side of the mosque. The mosque was built in 1710 by Ahmet III to honour his mother, while the wooden outbuilding was added later as an entrance to the sultan's loge. Female visitors will need to climb up a narrow stone staircase to reach the women's area on the second floor.

Şemşi Paşa Mosque

Pass out of the Yeni Valide Mosque into Balaban Caddesi. Bear left and follow the road towards the shore, ending up at the **Şemşi Paşa Mosque** ❺ (Şemsi Paşa Camii). This small waterside mosque is one of Üsküdar's most picturesque sights and another of Mimar Sinan's gems. Built in 1580 for its namesake vizier, it now houses a small library.

MAIDEN'S TOWER

Now take a left and follow the waterfront pathway about half a mile until you reach the boat terminal that shuttles visitors to the **Maiden's Tower** ❻ (Kız Kulesi; tel: 0216 342 4747; www.kizkulesi. com.tr; daily 9am–6.45pm, 8.15–12.30pm for dinner reservations only). Also known as Leander's Tower, it was built as a defensive watchtower by Athenian statesman Alcibiades. The Byzantine Emperor Manuel I Comnenus reconstructed it as a lighthouse in the 12th century, dedicating it to the mythical Leander, who drowned while swimming across to his lover, the priestess Hero. Now home to a restaurant, the isle is also a popular wedding venue.

To return to the European shore, return to Üsküdar Pier and take a shuttle from the Maiden's Tower to Kabataş, departing every hour (9am–6.45pm, thereafter 11pm, 11.45pm and 12.30am).

Yoros Castle, Anadolu Kavaği

BOSPHORUS BOAT TRIP

Follow in the wake of Jason and the Argonauts, who once sailed up the Bosphorus on their quest for the Golden Fleece, by taking a scenic boat tour on a quest for a fish lunch in the far-flung village of Anadolu Kavağı.

DISTANCE: 27km (17 miles) from Eminönü to Anadolu Kavaği
TIME: 1 or 2 days
START/END: Eminönü Pier
POINTS TO NOTE: If you are pressed for time, limit yourself to taking the scenic boat trip directly to Anadolu Kavağı and back. Due to the infrequency of ferries between various stops on the Bosphorus, the full extent of this route can only be completed during longer summer days. In winter you would need two days to take in the Asian shore as well. The weekend is the most popular slot with local day trippers, so make the trip on a weekday if you would prefer to sail in peace. The İstanbul Ferry Company (IDO) has a website in English from which you can download timetables (www.ido.com.tr). Should you stay in one of the waterside hotels on the Asian shore, a water taxi to and from the European shore will be provided. Just call in advance.

According to ancient Greek myth, the gravest task faced by Jason and his men was to sail their ship, the *Argo*, past the Symplegades, the infamous clashing rocks that guarded the passage from the Bosphorus to the Black Sea. They sent a dove before the ship, and it returned having lost only a few tail feathers, so the *Argo* followed, largely unscathed.

Trip highlights

These days, taking a boat up the Bosphorus is less perilous (despite some dangerous undercurrents), and is the best and most enjoyable way of seeing İstanbul beyond its bustling centre. The daily boats that sail the 27km (17 miles) from Eminönü to Anadolu Kavağı on the Asian shore afford an excellent view of the settlements along the Bosphorus, as well as waterside palaces and magnificent Ottoman mansions *(yalıs)*.

In addition to the ferry's last stop, there are many places of interest along the way. The ruined medieval fortress of Anadolu Hisarı and the nearby Küçüksu Pavilion are often unjustly overlooked, as is the pleasant village of Kanlıca, known for its yoghurt.

| Fried-fish stall | Great views from a deckside seat |

The Scenic Bosphorus Ferry leaves **Eminönü** ❶ every morning at 10.35am from the dock marked Boğaziçi Özel Gezi (additional ferries in summer; check timetables at the dock or online at www.sehirhatlari.com.tr). You can also pick up the ferry at **Beşiktaş** ❷ 15 minutes later. The journey to Anadolu Kavağı takes just over an hour and a half.

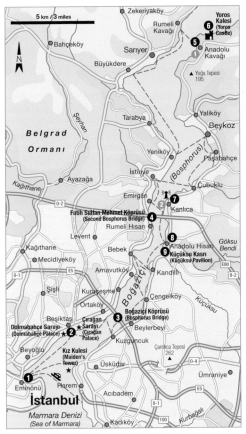

BOSPHORUS VILLAGES

As the boat leaves the Golden Horn, you will see Üsküdar to your right on the Asian shore, tucked behind the Maiden's Tower standing at the mouth of the Bosphorus. To your left you will see the stunning façade of Dolmabahçe Palace (see page 63), the Çırağan Palace (see page 65) and the village of Ortaköy (see page 66), before passing under the **Bosphorus Bridge** ❸ (Boğaziçi Köprüsü), one of two giant suspension bridges that cross the strait, linking Asia and Europe. Between the bridges, on the left, are the villages of Kuruçeşme, Arnavutköy, Bebek and Rumeli Hisarı.

After the **Second Bosphorus Bridge** ❹ (Fatih Sultan Mehmet Köprüsü), you will pass several other villages,

Bosphorus ferry

including İstinye, Yeniköy and Sarıyer on the European shore, and Kanlıca, Çubuklu and Beykoz (and swathes of military land) on the Asian side.

ANADOLU KAVAĞI

Alight at the ferry's final stop, **Anadolu Kavağı ❺**. Here you can have lunch and explore the village, which is famed for its fish restaurants. Be prepared to be set upon by touts, for whom the daily ferry landing is their indispensable bread and butter.

You could opt for a grilled mackerel *(uskumru)* sandwich to eat on a bench under a plane tree. Alternatively, go for a sumptuous meal of fried *kalkan* (turbot) or grilled *lüfer* (blue fish), with appetisers such as *midye tava* (fried mussels), *zeytinyağlı barbunya* (beans served in olive oil) and *haydari*, a delicious yoghurt dip mixed with garlic and parsley. **Yosun**, by the boat dock, is one of the better places, see ❶.

Yoros Castle
After lunch, walk to **Yoros Castle ❻** (Yoros Kalesi) on top of the hill behind the village. Originally a Byzantine fortress, the building was reinforced by the Genoese in the middle of the 14th century. From this vantage point there is a sweeping view of the upper reaches of the Bosphorus and the entrance to the Black Sea.

ASIAN SHORE

A ferry leaves Anadolu Kavağı at 3pm; in the summer months there is a later one at 4.15pm. The earlier boat gives you time to explore more of the Asian shore of the Bosphorus before it gets dark.

Kanlıca
The first Eminönü-bound ferry stops at the Asian village of **Kanlıca ❼**. Disembark here and stop for a yoghurt at a little café, the **Asırlık Kanlıca Yoğurdu**, see ❷, to the right of the pier. Kanlıca is renowned for this dairy speciality, usually sweetened with generous amounts of sugar.

The Bosphorus

A natural border between Europe and Asia, the Bosphorus (Boğaziçi; boğaz means throat) is a saltwater strait that connects the Black Sea with the Sea of Marmara. It stretches 30km (19 miles) in length, while its width varies from 660m (2,165ft) to 3km (2 miles). The predominant surface current runs southwards, but a stronger subsurface current runs at a depth of 40m (145ft) in the opposite direction. These deadly currents have meant that the passage has always been dangerous to shipping, but it remains one of the world's most strategically placed necks of water. Hundreds of supertankers and cargo ships pass through daily, bringing Russian, Central Asian and Caucasian oil from the Black Sea region.

Sailing near Rumeli Hisarı village

The tiny village revolves around the ferry stop where there is a small square, a couple of cafés and the **İskender Paşa Mosque** (İskender Paşa Camii), an unassuming building with a flat roof and wooden porch. Attributed to Mimar Sinan at around 1560, it was commissioned by one of Süleyman the Magnificent's grand viziers. Walk along the road south from Kanlıca.

Anadolu Hisarı

Continue towards the village of **Anadolu Hisarı** ❽. Sadly, the 2km (1.25 mile) stretch of road on this side is not nearly as scenic as its European counterpart, as all of the houses on the Asian shore were built on the water side of the main road.

Anadolu Hisarı is named after the **castle** that was built here in 1390 by Sultan Beyazıt I. It mirrors Sultan Mehmet's Rumeli Hisarı on the opposite shore, but is in a far greater state of disrepair and has almost melded back within the landscape that surrounds it. Nonetheless, the village makes for a pleasant stroll.

'The Sweet Waters of Asia'

Continue south from here and you will reach a small **bridge** that crosses the Göksu, the first of two rivers known to Westerners as 'The Sweet Waters of Asia'. Together they sandwich a relatively undeveloped stretch of meadowland, which was a popular spot for relaxation in the Ottoman era.

Küçüksu

Standing alone in the centre of this stretch, and named after the second, smaller river, is the **Küçüksu Pavilion** ❾ (Küçüksu Kasrı; Küçüksu Caddesi, Beykoz; tel: 0216 332 3303; Tue–Wed and Fri–Sun 9.30am–4pm; charge). Built as a hunting lodge for Sultan Abdül Mecit in 1857, this small palace is elaborately decorated with stucco, crystal and carpets.

Heading Back

From Küçüksu, you can take the no. 15 bus back to Üsküdar and catch a ferry to Kabataş or Eminönü from there; they leave every 15–20 minutes.

Food and Drink

❶ YOSUN

İskele Meydanı 1, Anadolu Kavağı; tel: 0216 320 2148; daily L only; $$
One of a shoal of fish restaurants around the main square, this is the most spacious of the bunch, with relaxed staff and fresh fish from the fishing boats docked outside. Try a plate of *hamsi* – deep-fried anchovies.

❷ ASIRLIK KANLICA YOĞURDU

Kanlıca; tel: 0216 413 44 69; daily 7.30pm–midnight; $
This wooden building next to the pier is *the* place to sample yoghurt in Kanlıca. Servings are thick and creamy, and come in various sizes. Copious sugar is advised.

Phaeton on Büyükada

THE PRINCES' ISLANDS

Catch a ferry out to the favourite weekend retreat of the İstanbullus. Watch the world go by from a horse–drawn carriage or trek up to a hilltop monastery for breathtaking views, then cool off with a dip in the Sea of Marmara.

DISTANCE: 14km (8.75 miles) from Kabataş to Kınalıada
TIME: 1–2 days
START/END: Kabataş Pier
POINTS TO NOTE: Ferries to the Princes' Islands leave from Kabataş Pier. If you have only one day, limit yourself to just one or two islands. Seeing all four in one day would mean an early start and a stay of approximately 90 minutes on each island to fit with the ferry schedule. If you have more time, you could spend the night at one of the hotels on Heybeliada or Büyükada (reserve in advance; see page 107).

Boats to the Isles

An hour's ferry trip to the southeast lie the bucolic Princes' Islands, known to the Turks as Adalar, 'The Islands'. This archipelago of nine islands in the Sea of Marmara has been inhabited since monastic communities set up here in Byzantine times; it was also used as a place of exile for deposed rulers.

Emperor Justin II built a palace on the largest island (now Büyükada) in the 6th century; it came to be known as Prinkipo, the Prince's Isle, and the name later spread to cover the whole group. Today, the islands' pretty beaches provide a perfect weekend retreat for İstanbullis. Cars are banned, and all transport is by foot, bicycle or horse-drawn carriage.

Ferries leave Kabataş approximately every 50 minutes or so (the first leaves at 8.15am), travelling via Kadıköy on the Asian shore to the Princes' Islands. They stop at Kınalıada, Burgazada, Heybeliada and Büyükada in that order, so it is possible to island-hop. There is also a fast ferry which leaves Kabataş once a day in the morning. Timetables are posted in the ferry stations, or you can check them at www.ido.com.tr.

KINALIADA

The smallest of the four inhabited isles, **Kınalıada ❶** is the first ferry stop. Despite its tiny area of 1.4 sq km (0.5 sq miles), with a winter population of approximately 1,000 inhabitants, the

Bikes for hire

Naval Academy on Heybeliada

island harbours some scenic walks, especially around its rugged south coast.

There aren't even horse-drawn carriages on Kınalıada, but nowhere on the island is more than a 30-minute walk or a quick cycle ride away. Climb the hill from the pier to see the **Monastery of the Transfiguration ❷** (Hristos Manastırı) and the fantastic view from its grounds. A holy spot since Byzantine times, the monastery was rebuilt by the Greeks in 1722, renovated again in the 20th century, and now serves as a holiday home for Greek orphans.

Halfway up the hill to the monastery, on Akgünlük Sokak, are the **Armenian and Islamic cemeteries** and the 19th-century **Armenian Church ❸** (Ermeni Kilisesi), dedicated to Surp Krikor Lusavoriç, Saint Gregory the Illuminator, the 4th-century founder of the Armenian Apostolic Church. Lunch options around the pier include **Mimoza**, see page 117, the most established fish restaurant on the island.

BURGAZADA

Only slightly larger than Kınalıada, the next stop, **Burgazada ❹**, nevertheless boasts five churches and monasteries, a mosque, several pebble beaches and some fantastic parkland for picnics. There is also a clutch of restaurants, including the vivacious *meyhane* **Barba Yani**, see ❶, near the pier.

It is worth making the climb, for the view if nothing else, to the **Greek cem-**etery and Hristos Monastery ❺** (Hristos Manastırı) at the top of Hristos Hill (head up from Çınarlık Sokak). Founded by Emperor Basil I in the 9th century, the original building lies in ruins around the current 19th-century church building.

Look out for the domed 19th-century **Church of St John the Baptist ❻** (Aya Yani Kilisesi) in the village on Yenice Sokak. Inside is an underground crypt, said to have been the cell of St Methodios, who was exiled in AD821 by Emperor Michael II for seven years, before returning under Emperor Theophilos to take the post of patriarch in İstanbul.

HEYBELIADA

Known as Halki by its former Greek population, the first recorded mention of **Heybeliada ❼** is by Aristotle. The second-largest island is a great alternative when the crowds on Büyükada become too much to bear. Consider staying the night at the beautifully restored 19th-century **Halki Palace Hotel** (see page 107), and taking a long walk around the island's 7km (4.5 mile) periphery.

The first thing you will see from the ferry is the **Greek Orthodox Theological School ❽** (Rum Ortodoks Ruhban Okulu; closed in 1971), situated in the Monastery of the Holy Trinity (Aya Triada Manastırı) atop Ümit Hill. The building was constructed in 1894 on the site of a Byzantine seminary.

Another scenic spot a short walk south from the town centre along Gem-

St John the Baptist church

ici Kaynağı Sokak is the **St George Monastery ❾** (Aya Yorgi Manastırı). Set on a cliff facing out to sea, this 16th-century monastery was once a refuge for residents escaping the plagues that swept İstanbul in the 18th century. Having suffered a fire in 1882, most of the original structure has since been restored.

Swimming opportunities abound at **Cam Limanı Bay** to the south, as well as at **Heybeliada Watersports Club** (Su Sporları Kulübü) on the island's northwestern coast.

The town centre offers a reasonable choice of places to eat; **Başak**, see page 117, behind the 19th-century **Church of St Nicholas** (Aya Nikola Kilisesi), is a favourite.

BÜYÜKADA

As its name suggests, **Büyükada ❿** (Big Island) is the largest island, and the most popular; the summer crowds can be overwhelming, especially at weekends.

Once off the ferry, check out the café inside the tiled octagonal **terminal building** (Büyükada İskelesi). Alternatively, if you are hungry, head for the fish restaurants lining Gülistan Caddesi, to the right as you leave the pier. They include **Ali Baba** at no. 20, see page 117.

A road leads uphill from the pier to the pint-sized **clock tower** in the village square. From here, you can turn left onto **Kıvılcım Caddesi** to browse the shops and eateries in the village

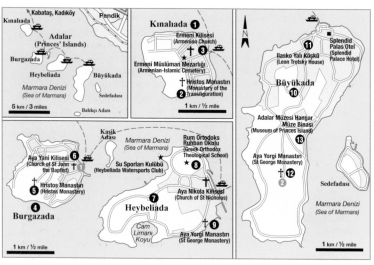

| Mansion gateway | View of Burgazada and Kaşik Adası |

centre. Otherwise, follow Yirmiuç Nisan Caddesi right towards the stately white-washed **Splendid Palace Hotel** (www.splendidhotel.net), with lashings of colonial flavour, and gin and tonics in the lounge at sunset.

Turn left at the end of Yirmiuç Nisan Caddesi, follow the road and turn right on Çankaya Caddesi, following it to Hamlacı Sokak. At the foot of the street is **Ilasko Yalı Köşkü** ⓫, a large late Ottoman mansion which was home to the exiled Russian revolutionary Leon Trotsky from 1929 to 1933.

Büyükada's biggest draw is the 10th-century **Saint George Monastery** ⓬ (Aya Yorgi Manastırı), especially during the festival of St George at the end of April, when devotees come in their hundreds. To visit the monastery atop Yüce Hill, you first need to get to the **square** at Büyükada's centre, where all the routes that cross the island converge. Either walk from south and uphill to the village (one hour) or take a *phaeton* (horse-drawn carriage) from the rank near the clock tower.

The steep path to the monastery is strewn with pieces of coloured cloth tied to trees. These are prayers left by believers who come to pay homage to the sacred icon of St George and partake of the healing waters of the *ayazma* (sacred spring) here. A small outdoor café, the **Aya Yorgi Kır Lokantası**, see ❷, has a sweeping view of the Sea of Marmara against the backdrop of İstanbul's skyline.

Before leaving the island, drop in on the new **Museum of Princes Islands** ⓭ (Adalar Muzesi Hangar, Aya Nikola Mevkii; tel: 0216 382 6430; www.adalarmuzesi.org; Tue–Sun, Dec–Feb 9am–6pm, Mar–Nov until 7pm; charge). It profiles the islands' history and heritage, through a fascinating collection of photographs, ephemera and artefacts displayed in an old hangar.

Keep an eye on the clock if you're not spending the night on the islands, and catch the ferry back to Kabataş.

Food and Drink

❶ BARBA YANI

Yalı Caddesi 16, Burgazada; tel: 0216 381 1375; www.barbayaniburgazada.com; daily L and D; $$

This popular Greek *meyhane* has a great view over the bay and a lively atmosphere, with live music in the summer. The menu is typical of a *meyhane*, with hot and cold starters, vegetables in olive oil (*zeytinyağlı*) and seasonal fish.

❷ AYA YORGI KIR LOKANTASI

Yüce Tepe Mevkii 5, Büyükada; tel: 0216 382 1333; www.yucetepe.com; Apr–Nov daily 11am–11pm, Dec–Mar Sat–Sun only; $

Choose from a simple menu of *meze* and grilled meats at this no-frills outdoor café next to the St George Monastery.

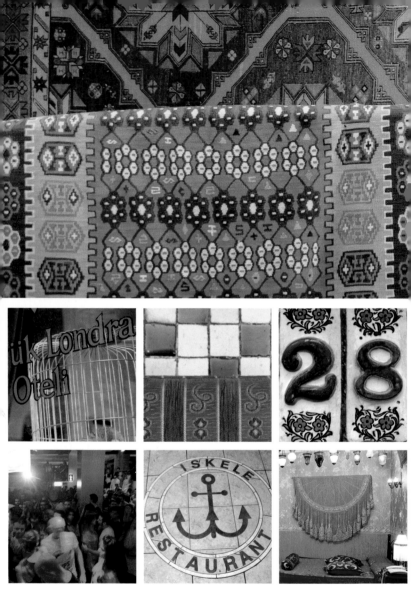

DIRECTORY

Hand-picked hotels and restaurants to suit all budgets and tastes, organised by area, plus select nightlife listings, an alphabetical listing of practical information, a language guide and an overview of the best books and films to give you a flavour of the city.

Four Seasons Hotel Istanbul

ACCOMMODATION

Choose between a five-star luxury converted palace or prison, bargain-basement comfort in a boutique hotel or an excellent mid-priced hotel, the latter found particularly in Sultanahmet.

When deciding on a place to stay, most first-time visitors opt for Sultanahmet, home to many of the city's historic sights. The Old City has dozens of guesthouses scattered around its cobbled streets, often set in picturesque Ottoman townhouses. However, as the area is so geared towards tourists, visitors are likely to receive the tiresome attention of touts and there is little to do in the evenings. An alternative is to stay in Beyoğlu, the modern centre of İstanbul (encompassing Galata, Tünel, Pera, Taksim and Beşiktaş), which is more convenient for the city's best restaurants, clubs and bars.

Sultanahmet

Adamar Hotel
Yerebatan Caddesi No. 47; tel: 0212 511 1936; www.adamarhotel.com; $$

> Price guide for a double room in mid-season for one night without breakfast:
> $$$$ = over US$300
> $$$ = US$200–300
> $$ = US$100–200
> $ = below US$100

The recent beneficiary of a complete makeover, the Adamar now boasts one of the best city panoramas from its roof-top restaurant. Rooms are spacious and colourful. All the main attractions of Sultanahmet and Beyazıt are within walking distance, yet the Adamar still feels slightly off the beaten track.

Alzer
At Meydanı 72; tel: 0212 516 6262; www.alzerhotel.com; $$$

The Alzer is a comfortable boutique hotel conveniently situated across from the Blue Mosque, with rooms ranging from simple economy to the Pasha Suite. Be prepared for noise from muezzin at dawn in the front rooms. 22 rooms.

Ambassador Hotel
Divanyolu Ticarethane Sokak 19; tel: 0212 512 0002; www.hotelambassador.com; $$$

In the centre of Sultanahmet, with views over the Sea of Marmara, the Ambassador is inside a restored 19th-century townhouse. It contains 22 rooms, two suites and a Turkish bath and spa with sauna. Breakfast served on the top-floor terrace.

Apricot Hotel
Amiral Tafdil Sokak 18/2; tel: 0212 638 1658; www.apricothotel.com; $

Büyükada hotel sign   *Les Ottomans*

New location for this inexpensive hotel with a real family atmosphere. The six simple rooms are of varying size; some can squeeze in four people. Some rooms have a small balcony for a little extra.

Armada Hotel

Ahırkapı Sokak 24; tel: 0212 455 4455; www.armadahotel.com.tr; $$

A reconstruction of a terrace of houses originally built for a 16th-century Ottoman admiral. Armada is located on a quiet street on the lower side of Sultanahmet, a 10-minute walk up cobblestoned hills to the centre of the Old City. There are views of Hagia Sophia and the Blue Mosque, and the hotel is home to two good restaurants and a bar.

Avicenna Hotel

Mimar Mehmet Ağa Caddesi, Tafdil Sokak 31–33; tel: 0212 517 0550; www.avicennahotel.com; $

The sheen is still on the satin cushions at this renovated hotel, set in a 19th-century wooden Ottoman house on one of Sultanahmet's quieter backstreets. The rooms, which are surprisingly chic for Sultanahmet, start from under $100 in low season. For a little more, you can have a view of the Sea of Marmara.

Dersaadet Hotel

Kapiagasi Sokak 5, off Küçük Ayasofya Caddesi; tel: 0212 458 0760; www.dersaadethotel.com; $$$

In a peaceful neighbourhood of Sultanahmet, this restored Ottoman house offers the luxury of en suite hamams in some double rooms. Service in this family-run guesthouse is impeccable, with breakfast served on the terrace. There are 14 rooms plus three suites.

Empress Zöe

Akbıyık Caddesi, Adliye Sokak 10; tel: 0212 518 4360; www.emzoe.com; $$

Situated near the Topkapı Palace, this American-owned hotel has 22 quirky air-conditioned rooms and suites. Traditional Anatolian themes abound, with kilims, embroidered bed covers and Byzantine wall paintings. The hotel has some budget singles and doubles starting at around $75, as well as large suites with *hamam*-style bathrooms at the other end of the price range.

The Four Seasons

Tevkifhane Sokak 1; tel: 0212 402 3000; www.fourseasons.com; $$$$

If you can afford it, this is *the* place to stay in Sultanahmet. A restored neo-classical Ottoman prison is now one of the city's most luxurious and prestigious hotels (see page 32). Wonderful views of Hagia Sophia and the Blue Mosque are complemented by splendid decor, all mod cons and top-notch service. Small and popular, so book well ahead.

Ibrahim Paşa

Terzihane Sokak 5, Adliye Yani; tel: 0212 518 0394; www.ibrahimpasha.com; $$

Hotel Kybele

Stylish and understated, this French-owned boutique hotel with a Parisian ambience is set in a renovated 19th-century Ottoman townhouse, next to the Hippodrome. The 19 rooms are on the small side and simply furnished, but friendly staff and excellent breakfasts compensate. The hotel boasts a spectacular view of the Blue Mosque, which is just across the road.

Hotel Ilkay

Hudavendigar Sokak 44-46, Sirkeci, tel: 0212 511 2270; www.ilkayhotel.com; $

It is hard to find accommodation as cheap offering cleanliness and friendly service, with simple rooms and a central location. It's a short walk to Sultanahmet and Eminönü, and the tram stop is outside. 60 rooms.

Hotel Kybele

Yerebatan Caddesi 35; tel: 0212 511 7766/67; www.kybelehotel.com; $$

A treasure house of Ottoman antiques and kilims in the centre of Sultanahmet, with a lobby lit by hundreds of old lamps. There are 16 comfortable, air-conditioned rooms with marble bathrooms, a restaurant and a delightful courtyard. English, Japanese and other languages are spoken by the helpful staff.

Mavi Ev

Dalbastı Sokak 14; tel: 0212 638 9010; www.bluehouse.com.tr; $$

The 'Blue House' is a truly charming hotel, located in a restored Ottoman house just behind the Blue Mosque. It's a real home from home, with friendly staff, simple but comfortably furnished rooms, a rooftop restaurant with spectacular views and free wi-fi.

Ottoman Imperial Hotel

Caferiye Sokak No. 6/1; tel: 0212 513 6151; www.ottomanhotelimperial.com; $$$

Right beside Hagia Sophia, this glamorous new hotel could hardly be handier for sightseeing. It's also hard to better the view from its rear courtyard which overlooks the old Caferağa Medrese. Traditionally decorated rooms and a rooftop restaurant complete a great all-round package.

Hotel Poem

Akbıyık Cadessi, Terbıyık Sokak 12; tel: 0212 638 9744; www.hotelpoem.com; $

If you are travelling with tight purse strings and are looking for a place in Sultanahmet, then this budget bolthole is a good choice. Situated in a renovated townhouse in the centre of the Old City, the rooms are basic, but clean and comfortable. What's more, the rooftop terrace affords some great views of the Blue Mosque and Hagia Sophia.

Sarı Konak

Mimar Mehmed Ağa Caddesi Nos.42-26; tel: 0212 638 6258; www.istanbulhotelsari konak.com; $$$

A beautifully restored family-run hotel in a Sultanahmet side street, the Sarı Konak boasts a delightful breakfast terrace with views of the Sea of Marmara. Larger suites are available in the building next door.

Sirkeci Konak Hotel

Taya Hatun Sokak 5, Sirkeci; tel: 0212 528 4344; www.sirkecikonak.com; $$$

Outstanding guest service is the main quality here, together with classically designed rooms, a small pool and hamam. Has two restaurants, including one on the rooftop with staggering views, and 52 rooms including one family room. Recommended.

Yeşil Ev

Kabasakal Caddesi 5; tel: 0212 517 6785; www.istanbulyesilev.com/en; $$$

One of Istanbul's most famous hotels, it is set in a restored, four-storey wooden mansion behind the Blue Mosque, and was once the home of an Ottoman Pasha. The 19 rooms have Ottoman brass beds and period furniture. Beautiful garden restaurant and bar.

Galata

Anemon Galata

Büyükhendek Caddesi 11; tel: 0212 293 2343; www.anemonhotels.com; $$

A restored 19th-century wooden house, with 23 rooms and seven suites, this boutique hotel is in a perfect position beside the Galata Tower. All rooms have outstanding original ceiling decoration.

The rooftop bar (venue for buffet breakfast) and restaurant have a fabulous view over the Bosphorus. Free wi-fi.

Galata Residence

Felek Sokak 2, off Bakalar Caddesi, tel: 0212 292 4841; www.galataresidence. com; $$

In the former home of the prominent Camondo banking dynasty, this apart-hotel offers various sized apartments with basic kitchenette and living areas. It's just a 10-minute walk from Galata Tower in a quiet neighbourhood. Good for families, and very good value.

World House Hostel

Galip Dede Caddesi 85; tel: 0212 293 5520; www.worldhouseistanbul.com; $

This hostel situated on a colourful street near the Galata Tower is a decent budget option. Bunks in shared rooms come at rock-bottom prices, but there are also tiny en suite doubles and triples available. The downstairs café is a popular backpackers' hang-out.

Tünel and Pera

Ansen Suites

Meşrutiyet Caddesi 70, Tünel; tel: 0212 245 8808; www.ansensuites.com; $$

This small hotel, in the historic Pera district just off İstiklal Caddesi, is an excellent-value choice. The 10 suites are elegantly decorated in a contemporary style, each with a fully equipped mini-kitchen and work desk. High-speed internet is available throughout, and

Büyük Londra Hotel

there is a fantastic French bistro on the ground floor. The penthouse suite has a view of the Golden Horn and a balcony.

Büyük Londra Hotel

Meşrutiyet Caddesi 117, Tepebaşı, Pera; tel: 0212 245 0670; www.londrahotel. net; $

The Ottoman-style furnishings are faded originals, and looking increasingly shabby although many rooms have been renovated. Rooms (non-renovated) start at $65, among the cheapest you will find in this part of town. The atmospheric lobby is full of Italian chandeliers, and the colonial-style bar harks back to the heyday of its regal neighbour, the Pera Palace.

Pera Palace Hotel, Jumeirah

Meşrutiyet Caddesi 98/100, Tepebaşı, Pera; tel: 0212 377 4000; www.jumeirah. com; $$$

Having undergone a major refurbishment fairly recently, this grand, elegant 1882 hotel, once the home from home for travellers on the Orient Express, was Istanbul's first-ever hotel. Rooms combine the elegance of Ottoman furnishings with contemporary luxury. Exceptional lounge on the ground floor for afternoon tea. See also page 55.

Richmond Hotel

İstiklal Caddesi 227, Beyoğlu; tel: 0212 252 5460; www.richmondhotels.com.tr; $$

On the pedestrian precinct of İstiklal Caddesi in the heart of Beyoğlu, the Richmond is a decent, if unimaginative, modern hotel within a renovated 19th-century building. The Leb-i Derya Richmond restaurant is recommended (for its sister restaurant, see page 113) and the top floor is a great spot for a sunset cocktail.

Taksim, Harbiye and Cihangir

Ceylan InterContinental

Asker Ocagi Caddesi 1, Taksim; tel: 0212 368 4444; www.interconti.com.tr; $$$$$

By Taksim Park, this hotel offers superb views over the Bosphorus and city. Luxury facilities include an outdoor pool, spa and gym, plus business centre, and restaurants serving Turkish, French and Californian cuisine. The 390 rooms include 54 suites.

Hilton Istanbul

Cumhuriyet Caddesi, Harbiye; tel: 0212 315 6000; www.hilton.com/istanbul; $$$

Set away from the traffic in extensive and tranquil grounds, this 1950s hotel is still one of the best in İstanbul, renowned for its high-quality service. It has 483 good-sized rooms and 15 suites, and has been fully renovated and lavishly decorated in recent years. There are seven bars and restaurants, and other facilities include a health club, spa and an outdoor pool.

Lush Hotel

Sıraselviler Caddesi 12, Taksim; tel: 0212 243 9595; www.lushhotel.com; $$

W Hotel   *Swissôtel hamam*

This turn-of-the-century apartment building in the heart of Taksim has been converted into a chic boutique hotel, where 35 compact rooms are decorated in styles that range from traditional Anatolian to Pop Art to maritime. It's worth shelling out a bit over the entry-level rate for additional room space. A sizeable buffet breakfast is served each morning in the ground-floor restaurant.

The Marmara

Taksim Meydanı, Taksim; tel: 0212 334 8300; www.themarmarahotels.com; $$$
The lobby of this long-lived and unmissable Taksim Square landmark may be showing its age but many rooms have been renovated – be sure to ask for one of the newer ones. The views on all sides are jaw-dropping, with an ace prospect of the square from the rooftop gym (and vice versa, of course).

Triada Hotel

Meslik Sokak 4, İstiklal Caddesi, Taksim; tel: 0212 251 0101; www.triada.com.tr; $$
The boutique-style suites in this 100-year-old building, just steps from İstiklal Caddesi, are stylishly furnished with hi-tech amenities and lovely bathrooms. Panoramic deck overlooking the city.

Vardar Palace Hotel

Siraselviler Caddesi 54, Taksim; tel: 0212 252 2888; www.vardarhotel.com; $$
This nicely restored, 40-room hotel was built in 1901 and is a fine example of Levantine-Selçuk architecture. A central location, good for business, shopping and entertainment.

Villa Zurich

Akarsu Yokusu Caddesi 36, Cihangir; tel: 0212 293 0604; www.hotelvillazurich.com; $$
With 42 simple and attractively furnished rooms over five floors, this friendly hotel offers fabulous service and good value. Set in the interesting neighbourhood of Cihangir, it's a short (uphill) walk to Taksim. Fantastic seafood restaurant on the roof terrace.

Witt Istanbul Hotel

Defterdar Tokusu 26, Cihangir; tel: 0212 293 1500; www.wittistanbul.com; $$
These 17 open-plan suites are superbly designed in a retro-hip style, with neutral colours and attractive floral motifs. Luxury extras include a kitchenette (not all rooms) with coffee-maker and microwave, leather sofa, grey marble bathroom, iPod docking station and free wi-fi. Great views. Highly recommended.

Dolmabahçe

Ritz Carlton Istanbul

Suzer Plaza, Askerocagi Caddesi 15, Elmadag/Sisli; tel: 0212 334 4444; www.ritzcarlton.com/istanbul; $$$$
The hotel towers above the Bosphorus with 244 tastefully furnished guest rooms, including 23 suites. It offers everything – not just a hamam, but

massage rooms for couples, and divine afternoon tea accompanied by a pianist.

Beşiktaş and Tesvikiye

Çırağan Palace Kempinski

Çırağan Caddesi 32, Beşiktaş; tel: 0212 326 4646; www.kempinski.com/istanbul; $$$

A superb hotel in a restored Ottoman palace on the European banks of the Bosphorus, the Çırağan is the temporary residence of many a visiting dignitary. The hotel offers a range of rooms and suites, some in the original palace. There are also luxury treatment rooms, an indoor and beautiful outdoor infinity pool, and excellent Ottoman and Italian restaurants.

Park Hyatt

Bronz Sokak 4, Şişli; tel: 0212 315 1234; www.istanbul.park.hyatt.com; $$$$

Perched on the edge of İstanbul's chic shopping neighbourhood, Nişantaşi, the Park Hyatt hotel is set in the elegant 1922 Maçka Palace, a building inspired by the stately palazzos of Milan. The rooms are spacious and the bathrooms sensational: a stand-alone bath, marble *hamam* basin and filtered drinking-water tap grace every room.

Swissôtel The Bosphorus

Bayıldım Caddesi 2, Maçka; tel: 0212 326 1100; www.swissotel.com; $$$

A steep walk up the hill behind the Dolmabahçe Palace, this massive all-amenities hotel with 600 simple rooms has a huge, lavish lobby. The service is excellent, and there are superb views of the Topkapı Palace and beyond, plus a wonderful outdoor pool and terrace.

W Hotel

Süleyman Seba Caddesi 22, Akaretler, Beşiktaş; tel: 0212 381 2121; www.whotels.com/istanbul; $$$

Near the Dolmabahçe Palace and port of Beşiktaş, what this hot new hotel doesn't have in view or location, it makes up for in its gorgeous Turkish-contemporary decor and über-chic glamour. If staying here will break your budget (although prices plummet off-season), then treat yourself to dinner at its Okka restaurant, or to a cocktail in the Sip bar.

Beyazit

Hotel Niles

Ordu Caddesi, Diekli Cami Sokak 19; tel: 0212 517 3239; www.hotelniles.com; $

This simple, spotlessly clean and exceptionally friendly guesthouse is minutes from the Grand Bazaar, and a short walk from the Sultanahmet sights. The standard double rooms are very reasonable, with recently added Ottoman-style suites and a duplex maisonette if you want to splash out. Breakfast is on the terrace café. Outstanding service.

Sarniç Hotel

Kucuk Ayasofya Caddesi 26; tel: 0212 518 2323; www.sarnichotel.com; $

A'jia Hotel

A good-value option in a restored town-house, with simple, attractive décor, a rooftop terrace and a decent restaurant. The hotel has the additional attraction of sitting right over a Byzantine cistern, which guests can visit.

Fener and Balat

Daphnis Hotel

Sadrazam Ali Paşa Caddesi No. 26; tel: 0212 531 4858; www.hoteldaphnis. com; $$

This small hotel was created out of a row of Fener townhouses across the road from an old Greek school. High-ceilinged rooms are wonderfully atmospheric, and the restaurant at the front overlooks the Golden Horn, albeit across a busy main road.

Asian shore

A'jia

Ahmet Rasim Paşa Yalısı, Çubuklu Caddesi 27, Kanlıca; tel: 0216 413 9300; www.ajia hotel.com; $$$

Located far from the city centre, past the Second Bosphorus Bridge, this small boutique hotel with 16 rooms in a former Ottoman seaside mansion is peaceful and secluded. For food, look no further than its elegant waterside restaurant.

Sumahan on the Water

Kuleli Caddesi 51, Çengelköy; tel: 0216 422 8000; www.sumahan.com; $$$

A super-cool boutique hotel in a converted rakı distillery on the Bosphorus,

this is certainly away from the busy city. Each of the 18 rooms and suites is individually decorated in a contemporary style with its own marble *hamam*-type bathroom. Half of the rooms have great views of the water with the Bosphorus Bridge as a backdrop. The rooms on the ground floor open out onto the hotel's garden at the edge of the water.

Princes' Islands

Halki Palace Hotel

Heybeliada; tel: 0216 351 0025; www.halki palacehotel.com; $$

The place to stay on Heybeliada, and the only decent-sized hotel here that's not a waterfront guesthouse. It's set on a hillside a 15-minute walk from the town centre, or a five-minute ride by horse and carriage *(phaeton)*. The 45 quaint rooms are good value, and there's a swimming pool for sweltering summer days. Book ahead.

Splendid Palace Hotel

Nisan Caddesi 23, Büyükada; tel: 0216 382 6950; www.splendidhotel.net; $$

This large white wooden building with red shutters overlooks the Sea of Marmara. The 100-year-old hotel retains its colonial feel, with the rooms arranged around a courtyard at the back. Although fairly spartan, and the floors a little creaky, the place is clean and welcoming. Try and get a room with a balcony.

Fes Café in the Grand Bazaar

RESTAURANTS

The majority of İstanbul's decent eateries are concentrated in the modern city centre, Beyoğlu; the streets that branch off the main drag, İstiklal Caddesi, are packed to the rafters with cafés and restaurants. Sultanahmet also has a few good places, especially around İncili Çavuş Sokak, although these are rarely frequented by locals. Fish-lovers should head for the Bosphorus villages or Kumkapı, while those with deep pockets could try one of the city's haute cuisine establishments in Beşiktaş or Levent.

There are many different types of restaurant in İstanbul; although the word *restoran* exists in Turkish it is rarely used in names. A *lokanta* is a simple canteen-type restaurant, suitable for a quick filling feed rather than gastronomic delight, serving *hazır yemek* (ready food) where you choose from heated trays of pre-cooked food. In the *ocakbaşi* the barbecue grill cooks sizzling meats on skewers. A *gazino* is a restaurant serving alcohol, usually with an evening floor show of belly dancing and folk music,

balık evis are fish houses and *meyhanes* are taverns.

The range of informal, cheap eateries is vast. A *kebapçi* specialises in grilled meats, notably kebabs served with pide (unleavened bread) and salad, while a *pideci* or *pide* salonu is a Turkish-style pizzeria, dishing up pide topped with minced lamb, eggs or cheese. You can enjoy tripe in an *işkembeci*, soup in a *çorbaci*, and milk puddings in a *muhallebici*. A *büfe* is a street kiosk selling snacks and soft drinks.

Sultanahmet

Balıkçı Sabahattin
Seyit Hasan Kuyu Sokak 1, Cankurtaran; tel: 0212 458 1824; www.balikcisabahattin.com; daily 11am–1.30am; $$$

A seafood favourite since 1927, this is one of the few restaurants in Sultanahmet where you will see locals dining alongside tourists. Choose from the leafy outdoor seating on warm evenings or cosy indoor dining during winter. The menu is in the style of a *meyhane*, with cold *meze*, hot appetisers and a list of the fresh catch of the day. Octopus salad and white cheese with melon are great ways to start the meal, and the shrimp salad is also excellent.

Doydoy
Şifa Hamamı Sokak 13; tel: 0212-517 1588; daily 8am–10pm; $

Price guide for a two-course dinner for one with a glass of wine (where available):
$$$$ = over 70YTL
$$$ = 40–70YTL
$$ = 20–40YTL
$ = under 20YTL

Kumkapı is an atmospheric spot for seafood

This is a long-time budget travellers' favourite which serves all the standard Turkish staples (lentil soup, a range of kebabs and baklava) at commendably low prices. The restaurant is spread over four floors and boasts a terrace with stunning views of the Blue Mosque.

Dubb
Alemdar Mahallesi, İncili Çavuş Sokak; tel: 0212 513 7308; www.dubbindian.com; daily noon–1am; $$

Located among the throng of tourist restaurants along İncili Çavuş Sokak, Dubb is a rare decent Indian option in the city. Chef Vinod Kumar Chouhan has put together a delectable menu from various Indian regions, with chana chat for starters, Kadhai chicken and Kashmiri rogan josh plus good-value meat and vegetarian set meals. The restaurant also has its own tandoor for grilling meat and making naan bread. Head to the top-floor terrace for the best views.

Karadeniz Aile Pide & Kebap Salonu
Hacı Tahsinbey Sokak 1; tel: 0212 522 9191; www.karadenizpide.net; daily 11am–11pm; $

Pide is the Turkish take on pizza, and this little restaurant that has been in business since the days of the hippy trail offers a great introduction. *Kaşarlı* is a cheese pizza, *sucuklu* is with garlic sausage and *karışık* comes with a bit of everything.

Mozaik
İncili Çavuş Sokak 1, off Divan Yolu; tel: 0212 512 4177; daily 9am–1am; $$

Next door to Rumeli, Mozaik is also a great option in Sultanahmet, with outdoor seating and charming waiters. Set inside a 19th-century Ottoman house, it has a sophisticated but relaxed atmosphere. The pastas and salads are good for lunch, and there's a range of Ottoman classics, such as lamb stewed with plums and the Abant kebab, with lamb chunks and sautéed aubergine.

Rumeli
Ticarethane Sokak 8, off Divan Yolu; tel: 0212 512 0008; daily 10am–1am; $$

With accommodating staff and a cosy interior, this restaurant serves an inventive mix of Turkish, Anatolian and Ottoman dishes. The *Saray Kebabı* (Palace Kebab) and *Portakalı Tavuk* (Orange Chicken) are the house specials, and the spinach-and-cheese pancake is delicious. If you have room for dessert, try the hot chocolate soufflé.

Seasons
Tevkifhane Sokak 1; tel: 0212 402 3000; www.fourseasons.com/istanbul; daily 7–11am, noon–3pm, 7–11pm; $$$$

For a real splash-out foodie meal, head for this rooftop restaurant at the Four Seasons Hotel, with magnificent views and world-class Asian-fusion haute cuisine. Reservations recommended.

Snack cart

Seven Hills Hotel

Tevkifhane Sokak 8/A; tel: 0212 516 9497; www.sevenhillshotelcom; daily B, L and D; $$$

Breakfast in the rooftop restaurant may not match the Four Seasons' brunch for choice, but the magnificent views of Hagia Sophia and the Blue Mosque more than compensate.

Kumkapı

Kör Agop

Ördekli Bakkal Sokak 7, Kumkapı; tel: 0212 517 2334; daily 11am–1.30am; $$

One of a stretch of old seafood restaurants and *meyhanes* in the city's old fishing neighbourhood (see page 37), 70-year-old Kör Agop offers decent fish meals at lower prices than in the town centre. Try the fish soup and enjoy the atmospheric sounds of the *fasıl* and gypsy musicians who roam the street, although bear in mind it's very much geared towards tourists.

Eminönü

Bab-I Hayat

Mısır Çarşısı, Sultan Hamam Girisi, Yeni Cami Caddesi 39; tel: 0212 520 7878; www.babihayat.com; daily 10am–11pm; $$

This five-room restaurant in a renovated warehouse in the heart of the Spice Market (but open independently) has a fabulous range of Turkish dishes, with particularly good meats and salads. Popular with locals, especially at lunchtime, it makes an ideal stop from shopping in busy Eminönü. Choose from the large high-ceilinged dining rooms, or cosy nooks overlooking the market's interior.

Hamdi

Tahimis Caddesi, Kalçın Sokak 17; tel: 0212 528 0390; www.hamdirestorant.com.tr; daily 11.30am–midnight; $$

A meat and kebab joint popular with tourists and İstanbullus alike, this family-friendly top-floor restaurant near the Egyptian Bazaar boasts spectacular views over the Golden Horn and Galata Bridge. A carnivore's delight, the meatballs are delicious, as are the chicken shish kebabs and spicy Urfa kebabs. Save room for sweet pastry *baklava* or *kadayif* for dessert. The service here is quick and not conducive to lingering.

Pandeli

Mısır Çarşısı 1; tel: 0212 527 3809; www.pandeli.com.tr; Mon–Sat 11am–4pm; $$

Up a flight of stairs from the entrance to the Spice Market (facing the New Mosque) is this dreamy turquoise-tiled dining room, with windows that look down on the bazaar below.

Karaköy

Karaköy Lokantası

Kemankeş Caddesi 37A; tel: 0212 292 4455; Mon–Sat noon–4pm and 6–11pm; $$

What was once the Estonian embassy is now a delightful turquoise-tiled restaurant that calls itself a *lokanta* and keeps alive the tradition of the *esnaf*

Lamb and rice dish

Bistro in Tünel

lokantaları (workers' cafes) by featuring a menu that changes on a daily basis. The dishes on offer are all Turkish, and despite its rather glam appearance prices are very reasonable.

Komodor

Kılıç Ali Paşa Mescidi Sokak 11/A; tel: 0212 293 5300; 11am–10pm; $$

Another newcomer to Karaköy's continually growing dining scene, Komodor serves thin crusted pizzas topped with ingredients sourced from a nearby town. The most popular pizzas are Milas, with Aegean herbs and cheese, Bolahenk, topped with goat's cheese and smoked tongue, and Hektor, with spicy beef sausage. Also a good place to stop by for a coffee made using a Nuova Simonelli Yacht Club espresso machine.

Beyoğlu

Agatha Restaurant

Pera Palace Hotel, Mesrutiyet Caddesi 52, Tepebasi; tel: 0212 377 4000; www.jumeirah.com; daily 7–10.30am, noon–3pm, 6–11pm; $$$$

The main restaurant of the Pera Palace Hotel (see page 104), this elegant dining room blends old-world glamour and refined modern cuisine prepared in a contemporary open kitchen. Dishes combine ingredients and influences from İstanbul, Venice and Paris – the three main stops on the fabled Orient Express route. With top class service, plus a huge wine list, this is the place for a real treat.

Boncuk

Nevizade Sokak 19, near İstiklal Caddesi; tel: 0212 243 1219; daily noon–midnight; $$

One of the multitude of virtually indistinguishable *meyhanes* lining lively Nevizade Sokak, Boncuk does vary slightly from its neighbours in that its menu has a strong Armenian influence and often a live band to add to the revelry. If you can, get a table on the street for maximum atmosphere if you don't mind the noise. Sample specialities like *uskumru dolması* (stuffed mackerel) and *topik*, similar to hummus but with added potatoes, onions and spices. Reserve at weekends.

Canim Cigarim

Minare Sokak 1, off Asmalimescit, Beyoglu; tel: 0212 252 6060; daily noon–midnight; $

There's no menu in this cheap locals' favourite, just off the nightlife hub of Asmalimescit. They just serve skewers of liver, lamb and chicken, barbecued on the grill, with piles of fresh salad and flat bread. Service is friendly and brisk, with no frills. Accept cash only. No alcohol.

Changa

Siraselviler Caddesi 47, Taksim; tel: 0212 249 1348; Nov–Jun Mon–Sat 6pm–1am; $$$$

Situated in a striking Art Nouveau building, the Changa is Istanbul's premier fusion restaurant. The consultant chef Peter Gordon creates dishes such as roast salmon with miso-coconut sauce

Presentation at Asitane

and duck confit with raisin pilau. Reservations strongly recommended.

Dai Pera

Yeni Carsi Caddesi 54, Galatasaray; tel: 0212 252 8099; www.dairestaurant.com; daily 10am–midnight, Fri–Sat bar until 2am; $$

A new cosy restaurant tucked away off İstiklal Caddesi. The friendly, welcoming atmosphere enhances the homely cooking created by owner and chef Arzu, who draws from her Armenian roots. Starters include flaky *borek* and delicious *mucver* (courgette fritters). For a main dish try the spicy *kofte* (meatballs) with red basil sauce. There's also a well-chosen selection of Turkish wines to sample. Popular with an arty crowd.

Fıccın

Kallavi Sokak 13/1–7; Beyoğlu; tel: 0212 293 3786; www.ficcin.com; daily 8am–2pm; $

There's no such thing as a free lunch, but you can come close with this place in the centre of İstanbul, where top-notch Turkish food is served at rock-bottom prices. Popular with the local lunch crowd, Fıccın offers a no-frills daily menu, with cold yoghurt soup, kebabs, *zeytinyağlı* dishes (vegetables cooked in olive oil), potato dumplings and *fıccın*, a meat patty encrusted in pastry. No alcohol.

Gani Gani

Kuyu Sokak 11, Taksim; tel: 0212 244 8401; www.naumpasakonagi.com; 10am–midnight; $

This *şark sofrası* ('Eastern table') is a delightful collection of small Eastern-style private dining rooms, spread over several storeys of a building in a hidden Taksim backstreet. You can choose from a room with a standard table and chairs, or opt for an oriental meal sat on the floor among Anatolian carpet-cushions. The food here is basic Turkish fare – kebabs and *pide* ('Turkish pizzas') – and no alcohol is served.

Hacı Abdullah

Atıf Yılmaz Caddesi 9/A, Beyoğlu; tel: 0212 293 8561; www.haciabdullah.com.tr; daily 11am–10.30pm; $$

This century-old option serves classic Ottoman-Turkish dishes like grilled and baked meats, stews and stuffed vegetables.

Hala

14A Cukurlu Cesme Sokak, off Buyukparmakkapi Sokak; tel: 0212 293 7531; daily B, L and D; $

A simple venue for home-cooked local specialities, especially *gözleme* (pancakes stuffed with meat, potato or spinach) and *manti* (ravioli) with garlic sauce. Located on a cosy backstreet, it's cheap and cheerful.

Imroz

Nevizade Sokak 24, Beyoğlu; tel: 0212 249 9073; www.krependekiimroz.com; daily noon–1am; $$

Imroz has been serving *meze* and fish dishes since 1941. If the street-side

360 restaurant, İstiklal Caddesi   *Zuma's terrace*

tables are full, head up to the terrace for a bird's-eye view of the tumult below.

Kafe Ara

Tosbaga Sokak, off Yenicarsi Caddesi; tel: 0212 245 4105; Mon–Thu 7.30am–midnight, Fri until 1am, Sat 10.30am–1pm; $$

High-ceilinged arty café owned by Istanbul's top photographer Ara Güler, with his works lining the walls. Enjoy an informal meal of ravioli, steak or just a coffee, inside or on the patio. Great for people-watching.

Leb-i Derya

Kumbaracı Yokuşu 57/6; tel: 0212 293 4989/243 9555; www.lebiderya.com; Mon–Thur 4pm–2am, Fri 4pm–3am, Sat 10am–3am, Sun 10am–2am; $$$

A chic rooftop restaurant on Kumbaracı Sokak, which descends steeply from İstiklal Caddesi. The effortlessly chic interior is bright and airy by day, and low-lit and romantic by night, with a view to die for from its terrace. The menu is a simple mixture of Turkish and international cuisine. Try the Turkish *meze* sampler, with fava-bean purée and stewed chub mackerel, before moving on to the slow-baked leerfish or its signature forty-spice steak.

Mikla

Hotel Marmara Pera, Mesrutiyet Caddesi 15, Pera; tel: 0212 293 5656; www.mikla restaurant.com; Mon–Sat 6pm–midnight; $$$$

Located on the hotel's sumptuous roof terrace, with Golden Horn views, the menu at Mikla reflects the Turkish-Scandanavian background of chef/owner Mehmet Gürs. He uses local ingredients in such imaginative dishes as 24-hour marinated lamb shoulder with pomegranate molasses. Summer evenings are divine, with the alfresco bar open late.

Sofyalı 9

Sofyalı Sokak 9, Beyoğlu; tel: 0212 245 0362; www.sofyali.com.tr; Mon–Sat noon–1am; $$

Hit the *meze* trays hard at this unassuming but intimate *meyhane* along Tünel's Sofyalı Sokak, a long-time favourite with local fish and *rakı* aficionados. Choose from more than 20 different types of cold appetiser, before moving on to the traditional hot appetisers and then the grilled fish or meat course. Highlights include the house special, *börek*, a pastry filled with meat or cheese, and the artichoke *zeytinyağlı* (cooked in olive oil).

Yakup 2

Çukurlu Çeşme Sokak 13, Asmalımescit; Tunel; tel: 0212 249 2925; daily noon–midnight; $$

When it comes to *meyhanes* (traditional restaurant) you don't get much more popular than Yakup 2. Founded in 1977, it attracts a devoted local following of chattering class types for its meze, which includes *ahtapot* (octopus), meatballs and fried liver. The grills

Iskendar kebab

to follow are pretty good too. Situated in a two-storey building, there is also a small veranda at the entrance, perfect for people-watching.

Zarifi

Çukurlu Çeşme Sokak 13, Taksim; tel: 0212 293 5480; www.zarifi.com.tr; Sun–Thur 8pm–2am, Fri–Sat 8pm–4am; $$

For a *meyhane* experience with an edge, head to the ever-popular Zarifi. Be sure to come at the weekend, when locals arrive in droves for the restaurant's Balkan- and Greek-inspired set menus (95YTL for a multi-course meal and unlimited alcohol) or cheaper à la carte options. Around midnight, the tables are pushed back and the volume of the live music (mostly local singalong pop) is nudged up a couple of notches, as the restaurant turns into a boisterous dance club. An authentic İstanbul night out.

Zencefil

Kurabiye Sokak 8, Beyoğlu; tel: 0212 243 8234; Mon–Sat 10am–midnight (kitchen closes 10pm); $$

A delightful vegetarian enclave with a garden, where daily home-cooked stews, soups and pies are chalked up on the boards, and delicious mulled wine is served on winter nights.

Beşiktaş

Kebapci Iskender

Suslu Karakol (Decorated Police Station), Yildiz Yolu 6, Ihlamur; tel: 0212 236 5571; daily 11am–10pm; $

Istanbul showcases every kind of kebab, from the cheap-and-cheerful late-night doner snapped up for a couple of lira to the perfectly cooked Iskender kebab served in elegant surroundings here. The Iskender kebab was supposedly the invention of a chef named Iskender (Alexander) from 19th-century Bursa. He stuck his sword into the ground and used it to cook thin slithers of lamb without charring them, then layered the meat into squidgy pide bread, added a dollop of fresh yoghurt, and dribbled tomato sauce and hot butter on everything. This is one of the best places to sample an Iskender kebab, dished up by a company that claims descent from the original Iskender.

Ulus 29

1 Kireçhane Sokak, Adnan Saygun Caddesi, Ulus Parkı, Ulus; tel: 0212 358 2929; www.group-29.com; Mon–Fri noon–3pm and 7pm–midnight, Sat–Sun 7pm–midnight; $$$$

Located in one of the city's more affluent residential areas, on a hill above the Bosphorus village of Bebek, Ulus 29 is the enduring diamond in İstanbul's culinary crown. Beluga caviar and fresh lobster are just two of the house specials, plus locally spiced luxuries, like kebab in a yoghurt sauce and Köfte 29 meatballs. At lunch time, the international repertoire extends to include sushi. The dress code is smart at this exquisitely designed restaurant, with a

Grilled fish at Eminönü

beautiful view of the Asian shore. Reservations are essential.

Vogue

Spor Caddesi 92, BJK, Plaza A Blok 13, Akaretler, tel: 0212 227 4404; www.voguerestaurant.com; daily noon–2am; $$$$

A haunt of the beautiful people, Vogue is one of the best places in İstanbul to eat top-quality fresh sushi. Its location, on the top floor of an apartment building a short walk from the W Hotel, affords beautiful views of the city, which are enhanced in the summer when the terraces open out. Apart from sushi, there's also an extensive menu of Mediterranean and international fare. Reservations recommended.

Lavanta

Mecidiyeköy Köprü Sokak 16; tel: 0212 227 2995; daily noon–midnight; $$$$

Housed in a rambling old house just steps from the water, Lavanta is the İstanbul incarnation of a restaurant that started life in uber-fashionable Alaçatı, near Çeşme. One of its biggest assets is that the variety of rooms spread out over the floors ensures that groups of all sizes can eat in privacy. The menu is international, the quality of the cooking superb.

Zuma

Salhane Sokak 7, Ortakoy; tel: 0212 236 2296; www.zumarestaurant.com; daily noon–3pm, 7–11pm; $$$

Zuma sits right beside the water at Ortaköy in a light-filled box of a building with a garden in front of it for summer dining. It has branches in London and Hong Kong, where it serves a menu that features not just the familiar sushi and *robata* (and sake, of course) but also some local specialities; in Istanbul these include sardines and bluefish. Food is served informally in a style known as *izakaya* that encourages sharing. Located in an upmarket part of town, right beside the Radisson Blu Bosphorus hotel, the Zuma is not a cheap place for a night out. If you need to keep an eye on the budget, visit at lunch time, when a set menu aimed at business travellers keeps the bill in check.

Adem Baba

Satışmeydanı Sokak 2, Arnavutköy; tel: 0212 263 2933; www.adembaba.com; daily noon–10.30pm; $$

An Arnavutköy seafood staple, Adem Baba offers a wide variety of fresh catches on a daily basis, including bluefish, black scorpion fish and mussels, while the house special of fish soup is served only on Sundays. The wood-panelled interior lends a jovial marine ambience.

Çiya

Güneslibahçe Sokak 43, 44 & 48, Kadiköy; tel: 0216 336 3013; www.ciya.com.tr; daily noon-10pm; $$

Zeyrekhane Restaurant

Three separate sites for this amazingly popular, good-value kebab restaurant with imaginative dishes from all over Turkey; vegetarians also catered for. Try for outdoor tables on the street. No alcohol.

Lacivert

Körfez Caddesi 57A, Kanlıca; tel: 0216 413 4224; www.lacivertrestaurant.com; daily L & D; $$

On the Asian side of the Bosphorus, near the Sultan Mehmet Bridge but with boat service from the European side, Lacivert is famed for its Sunday brunch. DJs provide music to enhance the ambience.

Lucca

Cevdetpasa Caddesi 51, Bebek; tel: 0212 257 1255, www.luccastyle.com; Tue–Sun 10am–2am, Mon noon–2am; $$$

Although it's a self-styled 'Bistronomique' lounge and bar, this chic arty venue is very popular with trendy locals. Come here for Med-American cuisine, tapas and lemon sea bass. House DJs play after-dinner sounds.

Fatih

Dârüzziyafe

Şifahane Sokak 6, Süleymaniye; tel: 0212 511 8414; www.daruzziyafe.com.tr; daily noon–11pm; $$

Housed in the former soup kitchen of the Süleymaniye Mosque complex, Dârüzziyafe is set around a pleasant courtyard leading onto a number of dining halls. The traditional Turkish menu includes a selection of soups, pastries, vegetables in olive oil and meats from the grill. There's no alcohol served here, so substitute your afternoon beer for a traditional şerbet (sweetened fruit juice).

Siirt Seref

Itfaiye Caddesi 4; tel: 0212 635 8085; daily 10am–11pm; $$

This welcoming restaurant is almost close enough to the Aqueduct of Valens to touch it, and has a roof terrace with a superb view.

Süleymaniyeli Kurufasulyeci Erzincanlı Ali Baba

Tiryaki Carsisi 11; tel: 0212 513 6219; www.kurufasulyeci.com; daily 11am–9pm; $

There are several small *lokantas* (Turkish-style cafés) on the site of the Süleymaniye Mosque, lined up along a street that glories in the unlikely name of Tiryaki Carsisi (Addicts' Market), after the opium-sellers who used to haunt it. The mainstay of these places is *kuru fasulye* (basically, baked beans), a popular Turkish staple sold here at rock-bottom prices. This is the best known of the *lokantas*.

Zeyrekhane Restaurant

Sinanağa Mahallesi, İbadethane Arkası Sokak 10, Zeyrek; tel: 0212 532 2778; www.zeyrekhane.com; Tue–Sun 9am–10pm; $$

Tripe is the speciality here

Kanaat Lokantasi's open kitchen

In a restored Ottoman *medrese*, a religious school once run by the nearby mosque, the main attraction of this restaurant is its terrace overlooking the Golden Horn. Zeyrekhane is out of the way, but worth the effort for views, traditional Ottoman cuisine and friendly service. Light meals include salads and *zeytinyağlı* (vegetables in olive oil), and main-course highlights include Kayseri-style *mantı* (meat dumplings with a yoghurt sauce) and the *beğendili kuzu fileti* (lamb chunks with aubergine puree). Good for lunch, or a summer's evening on the terrace.

Fener and Balat

Tarihi Haliç İskembecisi

Abdülezel Paşa Caddesi 315, Fener; tel: 0212 534 9414; www.haliciskembecisi. com; daily 24 hours; $$

Specialising in *kokorec* (tripe), this restaurant, established in 1938, is a shrine to Atatürk with photos covering the walls.

Üsküdar

Kanaat Lokantasi

Selmani Pak Caddesi 25; tel: 0216 341 5444; daily 7am–11pm; $$

An institution and much admired, Kanaat was established in 1933 and is a family concern serving time-honoured recipes. It's a step away from the Üsküdar ferry terminal. No alcohol or credit cards.

Trend216

Selmanağa Mahallesi, Selmani Pak Caddesi 1/3 (entrance also on Selmanağa Çeşme Sokak); tel: 0216 343 4410; www.trend216. com; Sun–Thur 9am–11pm, Fri–Sat 9am–midnight; $$

A no-frills local eatery, with great views over the Bosphorus and a decent brunch buffet on Sundays.

Princes' Islands

Ali Baba

Gülistan Caddesi 18, Büyükada; tel: 0216 382 3733; daily L and D; $$

A popular choice among the multitude of restaurants huddled around the pier, Ali Baba offers the fresh catch of the day accompanied by wine or *rakı*. Reserve at weekends.

Başak

Ayyıldız Caddesi 26A, Heybeliada; tel: 0216 351 1289; daily 7am–midnight; $$

Chef Abdullah Kuyumcu serves fresh seafare at this decent restaurant. Mackerel in soy sauce, shrimp casserole and deep-fried calamari are the house favourites, but leave room for the delicious baked *helva* (a very sweet sesame dessert).

Mimoza

Çarşı Caddesi 10, Kınalıada; 0216 381 5267; daily 9am–late; $$

Try the fried mussels *(medya tava)* at this modest waterside establishment, one of the island's oldest restaurants. There's a good selection of *meze* in addition to the daily catch, so ask a waiter for recommendations.

Bars and restaurants on Galata Bridge

NIGHTLIFE

Istanbul's nightclubs often have extremely high cover charges (on the grounds that Turkish females don't usually drink much) which may not be well displayed and yet appear infuriatingly on your bill at the end of the evening, especially is there is live music. The charge usually includes a few drinks however. Check before you enter.

The following listings are just a selection of the highlights of İstanbul's nightlife. For an overview of entertainment in the city, see page 20. Men travelling alone should resist the temptation to join a 'new friend' at his favourite bar or club; reports of pricey scams are still around.

Concert venues

Akbank Sanat
8 Istiklal Caddesi, Beyoğlu; tel: 0212 252 3500; www.akbanksanat.com
This small but amazingly diverse cultural venue manages to cram in a theatre, concert hall, cinema and dance venue to its small stages. One of several venues sponsored by a bank.

Atatürk Kültür Merkezi
Taksim Meydanı; tel: 0212 251 5600; www.akmb.gov.tr.
Formerly Istanbul's primary venue for classical and dance concerts. It has been closed since 2011 due to legal battles over a controversial restoration

project, part of the proposed development plans for Gezi Park that have caused riots in Taksim Square.

Balans
Balo Sokak 22, Istiklal Caddesi, tel: 0212 251 7020; www.balansmusichall.com
Live rock music venue with concerts and DJ-led parties in the heart of Beyoğlu. Check out their website for forthcoming events.

Cemal Reşit Rey Konser Salonu
1 Darülbedayi Caddesi, Harbiye; tel: 0212 232 9830; www.crrks.org
The resident orchestra puts on a diverse programme of concerts, including Turkish and religious music, and is the venue for several festivals (closed in winter).

Nardis Jazz Club
Kuledibi Caddesi 14, Galata; tel: 0212 244 6327; www.nardisjazz.com; Mon–Thur 8pm–1am, Fri–Sat 8pm–2am
This cool little club is the quintessential jazz joint in the city, with live bands nightly from Turkey and further afield.

Turkish Cultural Dance Theatre
Firat Culture Centre (FKM), Divan Yolu Caddesi, Çemberlitas, tel: 0554 797 2646
Excellent programme of Turkish dance from 10 different regions of the country, performed every Thursday night,

Babylon is a multi-purpose venue

including whirling dervishes and belly dancing.

Pubs

James Joyce – The Irish Pub

Istiklal Caddesi, Balo Sokak 26; tel: 0212 224 2013

The oldest and best-established Irish pub in İstanbul offers ceilidh dancing and live Irish music, as well as blues and African rhythms most nights. Imported Guinness and classic Irish pub grub. Very popular with foreigners.

The North Shield

Yerebatan Caddesi 13, Sultanahmet; tel: 0212 444 9332; daily 11am–1am

A chain of pubs around the city with a British theme, offering a good selection of imported beers and spirits. This one is within walking distance of the centre of Sultanahmet.

Bars

360 İstanbul

8/F Misir Apartment, 311 İstiklal Caddesi, Beyoğlu; tel: 0212 251 1042; www.360Istanbul.com

This top-floor restaurant and bar has a terrace for those jaw-dropping views and is a hub for the city's fashionistas. Late-night weekends see the dance-floor fill up courtesy of music from the resident DJs.

5.Kat

Soganci Sokak 7, 5/F, Cihangir; tel: 0212 293 3774; www.5kat.com; daily 10am–2am

Enjoy a glass of (pricey) wine on the terrace with Bosphorus views, or get cosy in the ornate interior. Early evenings are relaxing with jazzy music, but the tempo rises later on at weekends.

Badehane

General Yazgan Sokak 5, Tünel; tel: 0212 249 0550; daily noon–2am

Cheap beer and chilled wine draw boho locals to this tucked-away little bar in the heart of Tünel. Live gypsy music gets everyone dancing on the tables.

Hayal Kahvesi Beyoğlu

Meşelik Sokak 10, Taksim, tel: 0212 245 1048; daily 11am–2am

By day a cosy café, by night a live music venue featuring jazz and rock, with a young clientele. No credit cards.

Hayal Kahvesi Çubuklu

Burunbahçe, Cubuklu; tel: 0216 413 6880

Elegant, isolated summer spot for the well-heeled barfly, right on the water's edge but still in the city. In summer a private boat runs every half-hour from Istinye on the European side of the Bosphorus. The restaurant and café open noon–midnight, the bar until 2am, with live music after 11pm. Large dance floor. Sunday brunch 10.30am–3.30pm. Major credit cards accepted.

Leb-i Derya Richmond

6th floor, Richmond Hotel, İstiklal Caddesi 227, Beyoğlu; tel: 0212 243 4375/6;

www.lebiderya.com; Mon–Thur 11am–2am, Fri 11am–3am, Sat 10am–3am, Sun 10am–2am

Classy top-floor bar and restaurant with some amazing views of the city. Come for an apple or passionfruit Martini at sunset.

Pano Şarap Evi

Kalyoncu Kulluk Caddesi 4, Beyoğlu; tel: 0212 292 6664; www.panosarapevi.com; daily noon–1.30am

This quaint wood-panelled wine bar hasn't changed a bit since it opened decades ago. Come for dinner or just a glass from an extensive wine list.

Yeşil Ev

Yeşil Ev Hotel, Kabasakal Caddesi 5, Sultanahmet; tel: 0212 517 6785; www.yesilev.com.tr; daily 8am–11pm

The peaceful garden of this restored Ottoman house is a good choice for a pre-dinner glass of wine, one of few such venues in Sultanahmet.

Clubs

Anjelique

Salhane Sokak 5, Ortaköy; tel: 0212 327 2844; www.anjelique.com.tr; daily 6pm–4am

A chic and sophisticated club by the Bosphorus in Ortaköy, at its finest in summer when the doors and windows open up to the sea air and the night sky.

Babylon

Şeybender Sokak 3, Tünel; tel: 0212 292

7368; www.babylon-ist.com; Mon–Thur 9pm–1.30am, Fri–Sat 10pm–3am

Features an eclectic line-up of everything from local hip-hop acts to visiting rock outfits and folk bands. Check to see what's on while you are in the city.

Ghetto

Kamer Hatun Caddesi 10, Beyoğlu; tel: 0212 251 7501; www.ghettoist.com; daily 9pm–3am

Very close to the bustling *meyhanes* on Nevizade Sokak, this club, set in a converted bakery, is known for its live performances of funky Turkish and world music. Food is available in their on-site Metto restaurant.

The Hall

Küçük Bayram Sokak 7, Beyoğlu; tel 0212 244 8737; www.thehallistanbul.com; Thur–Sat 10pm–5am

This former shoe factory is now a pulsating multi-roomed nightclub, with international and local DJs.

Indigo

Akarsu Sokak 1–5, İstiklal Caddesi, Beyoğlu; tel: 0212 244 8567; www.living indigo.com; Thur–Sat 11pm–5.30am

The last word in clubbing in İstanbul, Indigo is the weekend home from home of the city's house- and electro-music crowd, with live bands and DJs.

Jukebox

Nizamiye Caddesi 14, Taksim; tel: 0212 292 3656

Anjelique is a great night spot in summer

With a spacious dance floor, this immensely popular club is a requisite stop for the best local and guest DJs. Usually packed at weekends.

Nuteras/Nupera

Meşrutiyet Caddesi 67, Beyoğlu; tel: 0212 245 6070; 6pm–2am

Located next to the famous Pera Palace Hotel is this rooftop club with great views. There are dance parties with local and guest DJs. Pricey drinks and a dress code

Reina

Muallim Naci Caddesi 44, Ortaköy; tel: 0212 259 5919; www.reina.com.tr

One of the hottest clubs in Turkey and more on the swanky side (be prepared for the high-flying prices), Reina is a vast complex dedicated to nightlife and filled with bars, restaurants and dance floors accommodating up to 2,500 people.

Roxy

Aslan Yatağı Sokak 9, Sıraselviler, Taksim; tel: 0212 249 1283; 6pm–3.30am

Trendy, expensive youth venue with great live international bands. No credit cards.

Gay and lesbian venues

Sugar & Spice

Sakasalım Çıkmazı 3A, Tünel; 0212 245 0096; daily 9am–2am

An all-day café and meeting point for the gay community, located off İstiklal Caddesi, cosy in the winter and with a small terrace for summer.

Tek Yön

Sıraselviler Caddesi 63/1, Beyoğlu; tel: 0212 245 1653; www.clubtekyon.com; daily 10pm–4am

A reliable favourite, this nightly venue features stage shows and a friendly mixed crowd.

Cinemas

International films are usually shown in the original language with Turkish subtitles (alt yazılı), though the title will be translated into Turkish. When going to see an English-language film, check that it's not *dublaj* (dubbed); if it is, Türkçe (Turkish) will appear on the programme listing or poster outside the cinema. This is usually the case with cartoons and films suitable for children. If you want to see the latest Turkish films with English subtitles, you'll have to visit during Istanbul Film Festival in spring. Popular directors include Yilmaz Güney and Nuri Bilge.

The Çemberlitaş (Şafak Movieplex, Yeniciler Caddesi, Çemberlitaş; tel: 0212 516 2660) is convenient for visitors staying in Sultanahmet, while Cinemaximum Fitaş (Fitaş Pasajı, Taksim; tel: 0212 251 2020) is located near Taksim Square on İstiklal Caddesi. The best shopping-mall cinema close to the centre of town is Maçka Cinebonus (G-Mall, Dolmabahçe Kadırgalar Caddesi 3 Şişli; tel: 0212 232 4440).

The Turkish flag

A–Z

A

Age restrictions

The age of consent in Turkey is 18, the legal driving age is 17 and the minimum drinking age is 18. Some bars and clubs will ask to see ID.

B

Budgeting

In general, accommodation and meals cost less in Turkey than they do in Western Europe, although prices have risen sharply in recent years, especially in Istanbul. Expect to pay from 100YTL (about $65) for the cheapest decent accommodation, twice that for a mid-range double and 800YTL ($500) for a night at the Four Seasons. A three-course meal, including wine, should come to around 50YTL ($30), but bear in mind that wine bumps up the bill considerably.

The cost of public transport is minimal for buses, trams and ferries (around 1.65YTL for a fixed-rate ride), and taxis are also inexpensive, at about 12YTL ($6) from Sultanahmet to Taksim or 40YTL ($15) from the airport to Sultanahmet.

The most expensive individual attractions are Hagia Sophia and Tokapı Palace at 15–30YTL ($10–20). Mosques

do not charge admission, but do welcome a donation.

C

Clothing

When it is hot, lightweight cotton clothes are the most comfortable choice, but evenings can turn cool, especially in spring and autumn, so take a jacket or sweater. Also take a long-sleeved shirt, a sun hat and sun block to protect against the midday sun. In winter, warm clothes and an umbrella will be needed.

Respectable clothing should be worn when visiting mosques and other Islamic monuments – long trousers or a skirt, long-sleeved tops and a headscarf for women. You may also feel the need to cover up a little when visiting conservative areas of Eyüp and Fatih.

Crime and safety

You are far less likely to be a victim of crime in Turkey than you are in western Europe and North America. Nevertheless, you should take the usual precautions against theft. One problem on the streets of Beyoğlu are solvent sniffers *(tinercis)*, who conduct bag-snatching and muggings, sometimes at knife-point, alone or in groups of two or three. Avoid badly lit, deserted streets at night and keep your valuables close to hand and out of sight. Report

Strolling along the Bosphorus

Tulip sculpture in Hagia Sophia's grounds

any theft or loss to the police. If your passport is lost or stolen, inform your consulate. Drug use and trafficking is punished severely.

The sporadic bomb attacks in İstanbul since 2003 have been mostly confined to embassies and far-flung outskirts of the city. That said, there was a bomb blast in October 2010 in Taksim Square. Nevertheless, the chances of being involved remain slim.

Customs

There is no limit on the amount of foreign currency that may be brought in, but no more than US$5,000 worth of Turkish lira can be brought in or taken out of the country. You can take the following when you leave Turkey: 200 cigarettes, 10 cigars, two bottles of wine, 1kg of coffee and 0.5kg of tea. Check www.gumruk.gov.tr for full details.

Buying and exporting antiquities is strictly forbidden. Should you buy anything old or old-looking, be sure to have it validated by the seller, who should get a clearance certificate from the Department of Antiquities. A reputable dealer can provide you with an invoice *(fatura)* stating its value and organise an export permit.

Disabled travellers

Few major sights have elevators or ramps, and wheelchairs are not permitted inside mosques. However, the new generation of green buses do have wheelchair facilities, as do most tram stations. The tram has a voice recording that announces each stop. All of the Metro stops between Şişli and Maçka on the T2 line have elevators. Disabled public toilets are harder to come by. There's a support association for the disabled called the Bedensel Engellilerle Dayanışma Denerği (www.bedd.org.tr).

Electricity

Turkey operates on a 220-volt, 50-cycle current. An adaptor for Continental-style two-pin sockets will be needed; American 110-volt appliances will also require a transformer.

Embassies and Consulates

Embassies are in Ankara, but most countries have consulates in İstanbul:

Australian Consulate, 16/F Suzer Plaza, Elmadag Askeroagi Caddesi 15, Şişli; tel: 0212 393 8542

British Consulate, Meşrutiyet Caddesi 34, Tepebaşı, Beyoğlu; tel: 0212 334 6400

Canadian Consulate, İstiklal Caddesi 189/5, Beyoğlu; tel: 0212 251 9838

Irish Consulate, Ali Riza Gurcan Caddesi, Meridyen Is Merkezi 417 4/F, Merter; tel: 0212 482 1862

US Consulate, Istinye Mahallesi, Uc Sehitler Sokak 2, Istinye; tel: 0212 335 9000

Fishing on Galata Bridge

Etiquette

Turks are by nature friendly, courteous and immensely hospitable – do not allow the persistent hawkers of Sultanahmet and the carpet-shop hustlers of the Grand Bazaar to skew your opinion of the country, as these irritating touts are very much in a minority.

Most important of all is dress. The majority of people in İstanbul dress modestly, and avoid shorts and skimpy tops even in the heat of summer. When visiting mosques, wear long trousers or a skirt below the knee, with a long-sleeved shirt or blouse; women should cover their heads with a scarf. At the Blue Mosque, scantily clad tourists are given robes to wear while visiting the mosque's interior. Mosques are open to tourists except during prayer times, especially on Fridays, the Muslim holy day. Feet are regarded as unclean, so don't point them towards anyone and remove your shoes before entering a mosque, or a Turkish house or flat.

You should never make jokes or insulting comments about Atatürk or the Turkish flag, or behave disrespectfully towards them (eg don't climb on a statue of Atatürk to have your photo taken).

F

Festivals

February/March: İstanbul International Independent Film Festival; May/June: International Theatre Festival; June/July: International Istanbul Music Festival; July: International Jazz Festival; September–October (odd-number years): İstanbul Biennial; October: Akbank Jazz Festival; November: Efes Pilsen Blues Festival and İstanbul Marathon.

G

Gay and lesbian travellers

Although the gay community in İstanbul has achieved some status of recognition over the past few years, homosexuality is illegal and a tricky issue among the common populace. The opening of several gay bars and clubs around the city has provided a good social grounding for gay men and women, but the city still has a long way to go to reach the levels of liberalism in cities such as London, New York and Paris. Public shows of affection are not advised. For a couple of venue listings, see page 121.

Green issues

Over 45,000 vessels a year pass through the Bosphorus Strait, many carrying oil, and marine pollution is a pressing issue for environmentalists. After a disastrous accident involving a Greek tanker in 1994, the government passed a new law trying to curb the transport of unknown hazardous materials.

Another concern is air pollution in İstanbul, and Turkey has been instructed

Fishing bait for sale   *Appropriately named boat on the Bosphorus*

by the International Energy Agency to increase spending on public transport.

Air travel produces a huge amount of carbon dioxide and is a significant contributor to global warming. If you would like to offset the damage caused to the environment by your flight, a number of organisations can do this for you. In the UK visit www.climatecare.org or www.carbon neutral.com; in the US log on to www.climatefriendly.com or www.sustaina-bletravelinternational.org.

H

Health

The main health hazards are the sun and the risk of diarrhoea, so use sun block and a hat during the summer. Drink only bottled water, eat only fresh batches of cold *meze* and avoid the *midye dolması* (stuffed mussels) from street-sellers in summer.

Healthcare and insurance. There is no free healthcare for visitors to Turkey. You should have an adequate insurance policy, preferably one that includes cover for an emergency flight home in the event of serious injury or illness. However, if you don't have insurance, Turkish hospitals are not prohibitively expensive, and they offer excellent treatment. They work on a pay-as-you-go basis, requiring payment on the spot in advance of any required treatment, including scans and x-rays.

Vaccinations. There are no compulsory immunisation requirements for Turkey. Up-to-date vaccinations for tetanus, polio, typhoid and hepatitis A are recommended.

Hospitals and pharmacies. The American Hospital (Amerikan Hastanesi) in Nişantaşı (Guzelbahce Sokak 20; tel: 0212 444 3777) is a very good, clean and efficient hospital with English-speaking staff.

There is a 24-hour pharmacy (*eczane*) in Taksim at the Aykut Eczanesi (Sıraselviler Caddesi 135; tel: 0212 243 1785), and a good English-speaking pharmacy in Sultanahmet at Divan Yolu Caddesi 26 (0212 513 7215).

There is a rota system whereby one pharmacist in every district – the *nöbetci* – stays open 24 hours for emergencies, and the address will be noted in pharmacists' windows.

Hours and holidays

Opening hours. Banks are generally open Mon–Fri 8.30am–noon and 1.30–5pm, while currency-exchange offices open daily 8am–8pm. The main post offices run Mon–Sat 9am–5pm.

Shops usually open Mon–Sat 9.30am–7pm. Many tourist shops stay open later and open on Sundays, as do malls and most stores on İstiklal Caddesi.

Museums generally open Tue–Sun 9.30am–5pm.

Secular holidays. Banks, post offices, government offices and other businesses will be closed on the following:

Seljuk tile frieze from the 11th or 12th century

1 Jan: Yılbaşı – New Year's Day

23 Apr: Ulusal Egemenlik ve Çocuk Bayramı – National Sovereignty and Children's Day (anniversary of first meeting of Republican Parliament in Ankara in 1920)

19 May: Gençlik ve Spor Günü – Youth and Sports Day (Atatürk's Birthday)

30 Aug: Zafer Bayramı – Victory Day (commemorates defeat of Greeks during the 1922 War of Independence)

29 Oct: Cumhuriyet Bayramı – Republic Day (anniversary of proclamation of the Republic by Atatürk in 1923)

Religious holidays. Turkish religious holidays are linked to the Islamic lunar calendar and move every year. There are two national religious holidays (Şeker Bayramı and Kurban Bayramı), which are marked by three and four days off respectively.

The worst time to travel in Turkey is during the holy month of Ramazan (Ramadan; dates vary from year to year), when the majority of the population (even non-devout Muslims) fast from dawn to dusk. This includes the intake of water and cigarettes, with the result that taxi drivers may put you out as the sunset approaches so they can stop to eat, many restaurants close all day or have very limited offerings, and people can, naturally, become more irritable. Şeker Bayramı (Sugar Holiday) marks the end of Ramadan, while Kurban Bayramı (The Feast of the Sacrifice) celebrates the substituting of a sacrificial ram for Abraham's son Ishmael.

I

Internet facilities

Wireless internet is becoming increasingly common in İstanbul, especially in cafés hoping to keep customers seated and drinking coffee for as long as possible. Try Gloria Jeans and Starbucks on İstiklal Caddesi. Internet cafés with computers are also available: there's Café Turka in Sultanahmet (22/2 Divan Yolu; tel 0212 514 6551) and a clutch of others around İncili Cavuş Sokak. In Beyoğlu, look around the small streets that branch off İstiklal Caddesi near Taksim Square; but be sure to look up, as they are usually located on the 2nd, 3rd and 4th floors.

L

Language

Around Sultanahmet and the main tourist sights, many people will be able to speak English, however it might be useful to know a few words in Turkish to get by. Locals will welcome any attempt you make to speak their language.

Turkish has several characters that are not in the Latin alphabet and which have their own pronunciation. Of the easier ones to get to grips with, the 'ç' character is pronounced 'ch' and the 'ş' character is pronounced 'sh'. The Turkish 'c' is pronounced like the English 'j' so that 'Camii (mosque)' is pronounced 'jami' and 'caddesi (street)' as 'jaddesi'.

Times of prayer at Beyazıt Mosque

The 'ğ' character is effectively silent. For some useful words and phrases, see the language chapter.

M

Maps

To get hold of any additional maps of İstanbul, ask at the tourist office in Sultanhamet Park. Another good source for maps is the İstanbul Kitapçısı (379 İstiklal Caddesi, Beyoğlu; tel: 0212 251 3328; www.istanbulkitapcisi.com), which also stocks a range of books about İstanbul in English.

Media

Television. State-owned TRT (Türkiye Radyo ve Televizyon) broadcasts a number of nationwide channels. News in English is shown at 10.30pm on TRT-2, while international sports events can be found on TRT-3. Many hotels have satellite television with BBC World, CNN and Sky, plus German, French and other European channels.

Radio. On shortwave radio you will get the BBC World Service and Voice of America. There are regular news summaries in English on TRT-3 (88.4, 94.0 and 99.0 MHZ).

Newspapers. English-language *Today's Zaman* and *Hurriyet Daily News* are both published Monday to Saturday, and offer national and international news and features. You can buy British newspapers at newsstands in Sultanahmet and Taksim; they are usually a day late

and expensive. *Time Out İstanbul* is a monthly listings magazine in English.

Money

Currency. Turkish currency is the Yeni Türk Lira (YTL; new Turkish lira), divided into 100 kuruş. At the time of writing, £1 was equivalent to YTL2.33 and $1 to YTL1.44. Coins are in 1, 5, 10 and 20 kuruş and 1YTL denominations. Notes are in 1, 5, 10, 20, 50 and 100 YTL units.

Banks and currency exchange. Banks are generally open Mon–Fri 8.30am–noon and 1.30–5pm. The most efficient banks are the Türk Ticaret Bankası, Yapı Kredi, Garanti Bankası, HSBC and AkBank. Rates of exchange and commission vary considerably, so it is worth shopping around. The rate in Turkey is always better than in the UK. You can also change cash and traveller's cheques at the PTT office.

Cash machines. A credit/debit card and an ATM is the fastest and easiest way to get cash in Turkey, and is cheaper than using traveller's cheques. ATM machines are commonplace in the city.

Traveller's cheques. These are becoming increasingly obsolete as a method of holiday spending, although they are generally accepted by middle- and upper-grade hotels, and by the banks mentioned above. Smaller bank branches may refuse to cash them.

Credit cards. Major credit and debit cards are usually accepted in hotels, restaurants, tourist shops and car-hire

Apartment of the Crown Princes, Topkapı Palace

companies. Some shops may ask you to pay a premium to cover the card company's commission.

Tipping. It is customary to leave 10–15 percent at restaurants, and to round taxi fares off to the nearest lira. A 10 percent tip to *hamam* staff is also appreciated.

Taxes. VAT, called KDV in Turkey, can be anything from 8–25 percent on purchased goods. Foreigners are entitled to a refund; for advice on reclaiming VAT on goods purchased, see page 13.

Police

Turkey's civil police *(Polis)* wear green uniforms. There is a police station *(karakol)* in every city and large town. The Trafik Polisi patrol the highways, and man traffic checkpoints.

To telephone the police in an emergency dial **155**.

The tourist police in İstanbul have their headquarters at Yerebatan Caddesi, Sultanahmet; tel: 0212 527 4503.

Post

Post offices handle mail, parcels and telephone calls, and often currency exchange as well – look for the sign PTT. The counter marked *'pul'* sells stamps. Hours are Mon–Sat 9am–5pm.

The main post office in İstanbul is in Büyük Postane Caddesi (turn left, facing the ferries, at the Sirkeci tram stop); other branches are in the Grand Bazaar and at Galatasaray Square. There are also small PTT kiosks in tourist areas where you can get stamps, post letters and buy phonecards.

Stamps can also be bought at tourist shops selling postcards. Post boxes are scarce, so try posting your mail from your hotel desk or at a PTT office. There are usually three slots, marked *şehiriçi* for local addresses, *yurtiçi* for destinations within Turkey and *yurtdışı* for international mail.

A 50g letter to the UK or US from Turkey costs 1.50YTL to send, while a postcard is 0.90YTL.

Religion

The national religion in Turkey is Islam – although officially this is a secular country. İstanbul also has Christian and Jewish minorities, and there are a number of synagogues and churches in the city. Details of local religious services can be obtained from the tourist office.

Smoking

Smoking cigarettes in enclosed public spaces has been banned since 2008, and a full ban on smoking in bars, restaurants and cafés came into effect in mid-2009. It was probably to be expected, in this nation of ardent smokers, that some venues – especially pubs and clubs – flaunt the rules.

Copper coffee pots　　　　　　　　　　　　*Stained glass at Sirkeci Station*

T

Telephones

The dialling code for Turkey is +90. For intercity calls (including calls to Üsküdar across the Bosphorus), dial 0, then the area code (212 in European İstanbul; 216 on the Asian side), then the number. To make an international call, dial 00 then the country code (44 for the UK, 353 for Ireland, 1 for the US and Canada, 61 for Australia, 64 for New Zealand, followed by the area code (without the initial 0) and number.

You can make domestic and international phone calls from public phones at PTT offices, or phone boxes on the street. These accept either credit cards or telephone cards *(telekart)*, which can be bought at PTT offices and at some newsstands and kiosks. Enquire about the discount phone cards which make international calls much cheaper. There are also private phone offices *(telefon ofisi)* but these are often more expensive.

Mobile phones. Turkey is on the GSM mobile network (North American visitors will need a triband phone). The three main companies are Turkcell, with the best coverage, Vodaphone and Avea. Buying a Turkish SIM card used to be easy, but it is now an increasingly difficult procedure. Currently, it is not possible to buy a card from Vodafone without having your overseas phone registered, which can be a tiresome bureaucratic process. You may have more luck with Turkcell.

Time zones

Turkish time is GMT plus two hours in winter and plus three hours in summer, making it two hours ahead of the UK all year round. Turkish clocks go forward on the last Sunday in March, and back on the last Sunday in October.

Toilets

Public toilets *(tuvalet)* are becoming smarter and more widespread. They can usually be found in museums and tourist attractions. Mosques always have toilets, although they usually charge 50 kuruş and can be quite basic.

Toilets are occasionally of the hole-in-the-floor variety, and sometimes lack toilet paper, so it is a good idea to carry a packet of tissues with you. Instead of flushing paper down the lavatory, put it in the receptacle provided (most places have a notice to remind you) as the plumbing can't cope. Some toilets are equipped with a special washing jet. Ladies are marked *kadınlar* or *bayanlar*, gentlemen *erkekler* or *baylar*.

Tourist information

The main tourist office in İstanbul is in Sultanahmet Square (Meydai), close to the tram stop (tel: 0212 518 1802/518 8754).

Turkish Tourist Offices abroad:
UK: 4th Floor, 29–30 St James's Street, London SW1A 1HB; tel: 020 7839 7778; www.goturkey.com

Boarding the ferry at Beşiktaş

US: 821 UN Plaza, New York NY 10017; tel: 212 687 2194; www.tourismturkey.org

Tours and guides

Official English-speaking guides can be hired through the local tourist office and through travel agencies and the better hotels. They are usually friendly and knowledgeable, and can prove invaluable if your time is limited. Free-lance guides also hang around at the entrance to Topkapı Palace and the Hagia Sophia, but don't let yourself be pressured into hiring one and make sure you agree on a price before you set out. Ensure, also, that they are authorised guides (ask to see their badge).

Transport

Arrival by air

The national airline THY (Türk Hava Yolları – Turkish Airlines; UK tel: 0844 800 6666; www.thy.com) flies to İstanbul from London Heathrow, Stansted and Manchester. Direct flights are also offered by British Airways, easyJet and Pegasus (a Turkish budget airline).

Turkish Airlines also has regular non-stop flights from New York and Chicago to İstanbul. For details tel: 1-800 874 8875. Most international airlines have regular flights to İstanbul.

Airports

İstanbul's main airport is **Atatürk International Airport** (Atatürk Havalimanı; tel: 444 9 TAV (828); www.ataturkairport.com) near Yeşilköy, 24km (15 miles) southwest of the city centre. A free shuttle bus links the international and domestic terminals. The airport offers currency exchange, banks, a post office, car rental, a tourist information desk, restaurants and duty-free shops.

Taxis are the faster and most convenient way of reaching the city, taking only 20 to 30 minutes to the city centre, and costing from YTL35 ($18). A comfortable coach service, Havaş, runs between the airport and the city centre, half-hourly between 6am and 11pm, with a journey time of around 40 minutes, although this is much longer during rush hour. Buses from outside the arrivals hall stop at Aksaray in the Old City, and Sişhane near Taksim, before terminating at Taksim Square. It is also possible to take the Metro (as far as Aksaray) and onwards by tram (connect at Zeytin-burnu) to the city centre.

Most low-cost airlines use **Sabiha Gokçen International**, Pendik, Asian side (tel: 0216 585 5000; www.sgairport.com), 40km (25 miles) from Kadiköy and 50km (31 miles) from Taksim. There's an hourly bus run by Havaş to and from the Turkish Airlines office in Taksim Square.

Green-minded air travellers may wish to contribute to the carbon offset of their flight (see page 125).

Arrival by rail

Allow approximately three days for the journey from London to İstanbul. The

Taxi stop on İstiklal Caddesi

InterRail Global pass allows various periods of unlimited travel in 30 European countries, including Turkey (for details tel: 08448 484 078; www.raileurope.co.uk). For route advice, see www.seat61.com. At the time of writing, due to work on the rail line west of Istanbul as part of the massive Bosphorus rail tunnel project, direct trains between Turkey and Europe have been temporarily suspended. Instead, passengers board buses at Sirkeci Station and are driven to the Bulgarian border at Kapıkule, where they cross to Svilengrad in Bulgaria and board a Bulgarian train to Eastern Europe.

The city's two main train stations are **Sirkeci Station** (Europe), tel: 0212 527 0050, and **Haydarpaşa Station** (Asia). The latter is closed to mainline trains until at least 2015 due to work on the Bosphorus rail tunnel project.

Transport within İstanbul

Akbil. This is an electronic transit pass, a small stainless-steel button on a plastic holder with a computer chip inside, available from kiosks in Eminönü, Taksim Square and other nodal transport points. It is an almost hassle-free means of paying for travel on buses, trams, the Tünel, Metro and ferries. Simply place the Akbil against the little circular socket at the turnstile (or at the front of a bus), and the fare will be deducted electronically. When most of its value is used up, have it recharged at an Akbil kiosk.

Buses. İstanbul city buses, whether run by the city corporation (IETT, www.iett.gov.tr) or private companies in accordance with city regulations, are cheap and frequent, but can be crowded, particularly at rush hour. Buy your flat-rate ticket or Akbil from a kiosk before boarding.

Dolmuş. A *dolmuş* is basically a shared taxi – a large (usually yellow) minibus that shuttles back and forth along a set route for a fixed fare. The departure and destination are shown on a sign in the windscreen. The driver waits at the departure point until all the seats are taken, then drops you off wherever you want along the way (*dolmuş* stops are marked by a sign with a 'D').

Ferries. For all ferries, buy a jeton before departure from the ticket desk (*gişe*), where prices and timetables are displayed, otherwise use your Akbil. Ferry timetables change from winter to summer; check www.ido.com.tr.

The main point of departure for İstanbul's ferries is Eminönü, between Sirkeci Railway Station and Galata Bridge. The jetty nearest the bridge is marked 3 Boğaz Hattı (Bosphorus Lines), for trips along the Bosphorus; next are the 2 Üsküdar and 1 Kadıköy jetties, for boats across to the Asian shore; finally comes the car ferry to Harem, near Haydarpaşa Railway Station, also on the Asian side.

There are also ferries along the Golden Horn, which depart from Eminönü, Karaköy and Üsküdar. A ferry at Karaköy takes passengers to the Asian shore.

Another major port is Kabataş, further up the Bosphorus on the European shore. Ferries from here go to the Princes' Islands and the Asian shore.

Sea bus catamaran. Sleek, modern passenger catamarans zoom around the city at rush hour, and out to the Princes' Islands (from Kabataş) several times daily during the summer. There are even Sea of Marmara routes to Yalova and Bandirma on the sea's southern shore for access to Bursa and the south.

Taxis. İstanbul taxis are bright yellow, and most are powered by clean-burning natural gas. They can be hailed in the street, picked up at a rank or ordered by telephone from your hotel. All taxis have meters and are required by law to use them. Most drivers are honest, but a few may try to rip you off by 'adjusting' the meter or doing conjuring tricks with your money. Fares increase by 50 percent between midnight and 6am. If you take a taxi across the Bosphorus Bridge, you will also have to pay the bridge toll. Few drivers speak English, so it is worth writing down your destination on a piece of paper.

Trains. There is a suburban rail service which runs from Sirkeci westwards along the coast to Yeşilköy near Atatürk International Airport. For the visitor it is only of use for getting to Yedikule. Buy a flat-rate *banliyö* (suburban) ticket on the platform and keep it until the end of the journey. The Marmary Tunnel (operational around late 2013) will link Sirkeci Station with a new station at Üsküdar via a submerged tunnel.

Trams. İstanbul has a very useful tram service *(tramvay)* which runs along the European shore, through the Topkapı Bus Station at the city walls to Sultanahmet, Sirkeci (Eminönü), across the Galata Bridge and as far as Kabataş (Dolmabahçe Palace). The section of line between Eminönü and Yusufpaşa stops at Sultanahmet (Aya Sofya), Çemberlitaş (Grand Bazaar) and Laleli (hotels). The tram is also useful for getting to the airport, if you change to the Metro at Yusufpaşa or Zeytinburnu. Buy a jeton from the ticket office and go through the turnstile, or use your Akbil. Trams run every five minutes or so.

For a map of the tram, metro and rail system, see www.istanbul-ulasim.com.tr.

A restored 19th-century tram runs along İstiklal Caddesi from the top station of the Tünel to Taksim Square. Another runs from Üsküdar down to Kadıköy on the Asian side.

Metro. Several lines of İstanbul's Metro system are in operation, and two are useful to visitors: starting in Aksaray Square, one goes northwest through the city walls to İstanbul's mammoth otogar (intercity bus station), at which you can board a bus to any part of Turkey. Another line connects Atatürk Airport with Sultanahmet (see Trams).

Funiculars. İstanbul's tiny underground

Mural in Gülhane Park showing the Sea of Marmara and Topkapı Palace

train, the Tünel, climbs the steep hill from Galata Bridge up to Pera. Trains leave every few minutes and take only 90 seconds to reach the top. A second funicular was added in 2006, linking Kabataş ferry port on the Bosphorus with Taksim Square.

Driving

İstanbul's public transport system, although by no means perfect, is sufficient for getting around the city on a short stay. Reckless driving and interminable rush-hour jams render hiring a car in the city stressful and time-consuming. The minimum age to rent a car is 21, and you will need your passport, a credit card and a valid driver's licence from your country of origin. Drivers from the EU, UK, USA, Canada and Australia don't need international licences to hire a car in Turkey. The four main hire firms in the city are Avis (tel: 0212 465 3455), Hertz (tel: 0216 337 0988), Budget (tel: 0212 465 6909) and Europcar (tel: 0212 254 7710).

Visas and passports

Visa regulations vary according to arrangements with different countries. Some nationals have to pay for a visa and others go free. UK, US and Irish citizens need a passport, and require a 90-day e-Visa that can be purchased online at www.evisa.gov.tr. The cost is US$20 (£13).

W

Websites

Useful websites include:

www.mymerhaba.com – a bible for expats, this site has extensive information useful for long-term visitors.

www.istanbul.com – useful and well laid out, this site is supported by the tourist board and features plenty of ideas and information about the city.

www.biletix.com – Ticketmaster's Turkish branch is a great source for concert information in the city and buying tickets online.

www.kultur.gov.tr – the Ministry of Culture and Tourism.

Women travellers

İstanbul is generally a safe place for women to travel, although harassment in tourist areas can be an irritation. A woman accompanied by a man is less likely to attract unwanted attention, but is not immune. The best strategy is to dress modestly, with trousers or a long skirt, and a long-sleeved, loose-fitting top. Walk with purpose and avoid eye contact. People will generally accept a firm 'no' and don't feel obliged to make conversation if you feel uncomfortable. Politely but firmly refuse all unwanted offers. If necessary, raise your voice and a dozen knights in shining armour will rush to your aid. Treating women dishonourably is an offence to Islam and will not be tolerated by the locals.

Arabic script in the Black Eunuchs courtyard, Topkapı Palace

LANGUAGE

For most visitors Turkish is not an easy language to pick up mainly because the vocabulary largely derives from Arabic and Farsi. Grammatically it is also bamboozling for English speakers because the verb goes at the end of the sentence and carries a series of suffixes to represent tense and person. But if you can manage even half a dozen words Turks will be appreciative. Most Turks who work in tourism speak excellent English as well as multiple other languages.

Basics

Hello *Merhaba*
Good morning *Günaydın*
Good day *İyi günler*
Good evening *İyi akşamlar*
Goodbye *Hoşçakalın*
How are you? *Nasılsınız?*
Fine, thanks *İyiyim, teşekkürler*
Excuse me (attention) *Aferdersiniz*
Sorry *Özür dilerim*
Yes/no *Evet/hayır*
Please *Lütfen*
Thank you *Teşekkür ederim*
You're welcome *Bir şey değil*
What's your name? *İsminiz nedir?*
My name is... *İsmim...*
Where are you from? *Nerelisiniz?*
I'm from the US/UK *Amerikadanım/ Birleşik Krallıktanım*
I'd like... *...istiyorum*
I don't like... *Sevmiyorum...*
OK *Tamam*

Communications

Where's an internet café? *İnternet kafe nerede?*
Can I access the internet here? *Burada internete girebilir?*
How much per hour/half hour? *Saati/ Yarım saati ne kadar?*
Does it have wireless internet? *Kablosuz internet var mı?*
What is the WiFi password? *Kablosuz ağın şifresi nedir?*
Are you on Facebook/Twitter? *Facebook/Twitter'da mısın?*

Emergencies

Help! *İmdat!*
Call a doctor/the police/an ambulance *Doktor/polis/ambulans çağırınız*
I'm lost *Kayboldum*
Hospital *Hastane*
Pharmacist *Eczane*
Police station *Karakol*

Health

I'm ill *Hastayım*
I'm allergic to... *...alerjim var*
Antiseptic *Antiseptik*
Antibiotics *Antibiyotik*
Aspirin *Aspirin*
Contraceptives *Prezervatif*
Diarrhoea *İshali*
Headache *Başım ağrıyor*
Medicine *İlaç*
Suncream *Güneş kremi*
Tampons *Tampon*

Çarşi Kapı Gate into the Grand Bazaar

In a restaurant

Can I have the menu please? *Menüyü lütfen?*
The bill please *Hesap lütfen*
I don't eat meat *Hiç et yemiyorum*
I'd like... ... *istiyorum*
Cheers! *Şerefe!*
Knife *Bıcak*
Fork *Çatal*
Spoon *Kaşık*
Plate *Tabak*
Wine glass *Kadeh*
Where is the toilet? *Tuvalet nerede?*

Language difficulties

Do you speak English? *İngilizçe konuşuyor musunuz?*
I don't speak Turkish *Türkçe konuşmuyorum*
Could you repeat that? *Tekrar eder misiniz?*
I don't understand *Anlamıyorum/anlamadım*
I understand *Anlıyorum/anladım*

Numbers

One *Bir*
Two *İki*
Three *Üç*
Four *Dört*
Five *Beş*
Six *Altı*
Seven *Yedi*
Eight *Sekiz*
Nine *Dokuz*
Ten *On*
Eleven *Onbir*
Twelve *Oniki*

Twenty *Yirmi*
Thirty *Otuz*
Forty *Kırk*
Fifty *Elli*
Sixty *Altmış*
Seventy *Yetmiş*
Eighty *Seksen*
Ninety *Doksan*
One hundred *Yüz*

Shopping

Do you have...? *... var mı?*
We don't have it *Yok*
How much is this? *Ne kadar?/kaç para?*
It's too expensive *Pahalı*
Can I look at it? *Bakabilir miyim?*
Can I taste it? *Tadabilir miyim?*
Open *Açık*
Closed *Kapalı*

Sightseeing

Where is...? *...nerede?*
Mosque *Camii*
Museum *Müze*
Palace *Saray*
Tourism office *Turizm Danısma Bürosu*
Entrance *Giriş*
Exit *Çıkış*

Transport

Bus *Otobüs*
Bus station *Otogar*
Ferry *Vapur/feribot*
Landing stage *İskele*
Ticket *Bilet*
Train *Tren*
Train station *Gar*
Tram *Tramvay*

Old Book Bazaar in Beyazıt

BOOKS AND FILM

Books

In 2006 Turkish literature received a big shot in the arm when the İstanbul-born writer Orhan Pamuk won the Nobel Prize for Literature. Although relatively few Turks are regular readers, traditionally they have held writers, particularly poets, in considerable regard and the city is dotted with memorials to its authors. The sudden switch from use of the Arabic alphabet to the Latin alphabet in 1928 cut most of the population off from Ottoman Turkish literature. However, a growing number of modern Turkish novels and poems are being translated into English.

Contemporary Turkish novelists

With the exception of *Snow* which was set in remote Kars, **Orhan Pamuk**'s books are inextricably bound up with life in İstanbul, and with the exception of *My Name Is Red* with modern İstanbul at that. Few of them make for easy reads although his stories of the goings-on amongst 16th-century calligraphers in *My Name Is Red* gave a new twist to the detective story. Roaring up behind Pamuk in the fame stakes comes **Elif Şafak** whose *The Bastard of İstanbul* saw her charged, like Pamuk before her, with 'insulting Turkishness'. Both authors were eventually acquitted and Şafak has gone on to pen *The Forty Rules of Love*, a remarkable retelling of the story of Celaleddin Rumi (Mevlana).

Tipped for the Nobel prize before Pamuk beat him to it was **Yaşar Kemal**, most of whose novels deal with life in the Çukurova region near Adana although a couple – *The Sea-Crossed Fishermen* and *The Birds are Also Gone* – are also set in İstanbul.

Other writers to look out for include **Buket Uzuner** whose most recent novel *İstanbullu* was set in the airport, and **Ayşe Kulin** whose *Farewell* is set against a backdrop of the British occupation of the city in 1923.

Turkish poets

The grand old man of Turkish poetry is **Nazım Hikmet** (1902–63) who spent much of his life in prison as a Communist and died in exile in Russia where he was buried. Other poets who have left their mark on the city include **Bedri Rahmi Eyüboğlu** (1913–75) whose wonderful *Ballad of İstanbul* will win over even non-poetry-lovers; **Orhan Veli** (1914–50) whose statue looks out over the Bosphorus just before Rumeli Hisarı; and **Tevfik Fikret** (1867–1915) whose lovely house at Aşiyan, near Rumeli Hisarı, is open to the public.

Turkish memoirs

As well as his novels Orhan Pamuk has written *İstanbul: Memoirs of a City*, an

atmospheric evocation of the city of his youth. But for many the most poignant of all accounts of the city will be **İrfan Olga**'s heart-rending retelling of his family's collapse into poverty in the aftermath of the Turkish War of Independence in *Portrait of an İstanbul Family*.

Foreign writers

A number of foreign writers have taken inspiration from the city. American Maureen Freely's novel *Enlightenment* looks at left-wing activism in 1970s İstanbul. The French traveller pen-named Pierre Loti (1850–1923) has a café named after him at Eyüp where he carried on the romance that inspired his novel *Ayizade*. British-born writers Barbara Nadel (whose books feature the chain-smoking Inspector İkmen) and Jason Goodwin (who created the eunuch investigator Yashim in *The Janissary Tree*) have set crime stories here. German-born but American-raised Jenny White has written a crime trilogy featuring a romantically-minded magistrate called Kamil Pasha. In *The Bridge*, by Geert Mak, Istanbul's Galata Bridge and its often louche social milieu is the starting point for a brilliant, alternative summary of the city around it. Mak uses life around the bridge as a metaphor for the wider country.

Foreign travel writers have written some memorable accounts of İstanbul, including *Innocents Abroad* by Mark Twain (1835-1910). Orhan Pamuk's favourite account of the city is the 19th-century Edmondo de Amicis' *Constantinople*. More recent accounts include Jeremy Seal's *A Fez of the Heart* and Tim Kelsey's *Dervish*. Finally, Brendan Shanahan's *In Turkey I Am Beautiful* concentrates on eastern Turkey.

Poets who have made the city their home include the American John Ash (*The Parthian Stones*). Also American, Paulann Petersen's poems touch on subjects such as the Four Seasons Hotel and a *nargile* café in *Blood Silk*.

Film

Turkish cinema has been on a roll recently with directors like Nuri Bilge Ceylan finding international success with films such as *Üç Maymun* ('Three Monkeys'). Other names to conjure with include Ferzan Özpetek whose 1997 film *Hamam* ('Steam') was a critical and commercial success, and Çağan Irmak whose 2008 film *Issız Adam* ('Alone') was almost as popular for its soundtrack as for its script. Although Turkey does produce some action movies such as 2004's *Kurtlar Vadisi Iraq*, a spin-off from a popular TV series, and comedies such as 2006's *Dondurmam Gaymak* ('Ice Cream I Scream'), most of its output is heavy on drama and sentiment with a liberal helping of politics, a tradition largely established by the much revered Yılmaz Güney whose *Yol* ('The Way') won the Palme d'Or at the Cannes Film Festival in 1982.

ABOUT THIS BOOK

This *Explore Guide* has been produced by the editors of Insight Guides, whose books have set the standard for visual travel guides since 1970. With top-quality photography and authoritative recommendations, these guidebooks bring you the very best routes and itineraries in the world's most exciting destinations.

BEST ROUTES

The routes in the book provide something to suit all budgets, tastes and trip lengths. As well as covering the destination's many classic attractions, the itineraries track lesser-known sights, and there are also excursions for those who want to extend their visit outside the city centre. The routes embrace a range of interests, so whether you are an art fan, a gourmet, a history buff or have kids to entertain, you will find an option to suit.

We recommend reading the whole of a route before setting out. This should help you to familiarise yourself with it and enable you to plan where to stop for refreshments – options are shown in the 'Food and Drink' box at the end of each tour.

For our pick of the tours by theme, consult Recommended Routes for… (see pages 4–5).

INTRODUCTION

The routes are set in context by this introductory section, giving an overview of the destination to set the scene, plus background information on food and drink, shopping and more, while a succinct history timeline highlights the key events over the centuries.

DIRECTORY

Also supporting the routes is a Directory chapter, with a clearly organised A–Z of practical information, our pick of where to stay while you are there and select restaurant listings; these eateries complement the more low-key cafés and restaurants that feature within the routes and are intended to offer a wider choice for evening dining. Also included here are some nightlife listings, plus a handy language guide and our recommendations for books and films about the destination.

ABOUT THE AUTHORS

Emma Levine is a writer and photographer who loved İstanbul so much when she first visited, she subsequently moved there. Now based in London, Emma still writes frequently on the city and Turkish culture, as well as following the fortunes of her one-time local soccer team, Beşiktaş. This guide builds on original content by author and photographer Vanessa Able, who has been writing about İstanbul since she moved to the city in 2005. Thanks also go to Jackie Staddon and Hilary Weston.

CONTACT THE EDITORS

We hope you find this Explore Guide useful, interesting and a pleasure to read. If you have any questions or feedback on the text, pictures or maps, please do let us know. If you have noticed any errors or outdated facts, or have suggestions for places to include on the routes, we would be delighted to hear from you. Please drop us an email at insight@apaguide.co.uk. Thanks!

CREDITS

Explore Istanbul
Contributors: Emma Levine
Commissioning Editor: Catherine Dreghorn
Series Editor: Sarah Clark
Art Editor: Zoe Goodwin
Map Production: original cartography
Berndston and Berndston, updated by Apa
Cartography Department
Production: Tynan Dean and Rebeka Davies

Photo credits: 4Corners Images 42; A'jia
Hotel 106/107; akg-images 24; Anjelique
121; Asitane Restaurant 112; Axiom 118;
Four Seasons 28/29, 32, 100; Getty Images
22, 119; Ghetto 20; indigo/mika organiza-
tion 98ML, 120; iStockphoto 2MR, 2ML, 10,
40, 73, 76/77, 96, 97L, 110L, 110/111;
Kebapci Iskender 114; Kempinski Hotel
103; Klub Karoke 21T; Kybele Hotel 98MR,
102; Leonardo 105L; Marcus Wilson Smith/
Apa Publications 6MR, 6/7T, 28; Mary
Evans Picture Library 25; Nardis Jazz Club
21B; Phil Wood/Apa Publications 62/63;
Public Domain 116/117; Rebecca Erol/Apa
Publications 1, 2ML, 2MC, 2MR, 2MC, 2/3T,
4/5(all), 6ML, 6MC, 6ML, 6MC, 6MR, 8, 9T,
9B, 10/11T, 11B 11T, 12, 13, 14, 14/15,
16, 17T, 17B, 18T, 18B, 19, 22/23, 23L,
26/27(all), 29L, 30, 32/33, 33L, 34, 34/35,
35L, 36, 37, 38, 38/39, 39L, 40/41, 41L,
43, 44, 44/45, 45L, 46, 46/47, 47L, 48/49,
50, 50/51, 51L, 52, 52/53, 53L, 54, 55, 56,
57, 58, 59, 60, 61, 62, 63L, 64/65(all), 66,
67, 68, 69L, 68/69, 70, 70/71, 71L, 72T,
72B, 74, 75L, 74/75, 77L, 78, 78/79, 79L,
80, 80/81, 81L, 82, 83, 84, 85, 86, 86/87,
87L, 88, 88/89, 89L, 90L, 90/91, 92, 93,
94, 94/95, 95L, 96/97, 98ML, 98MC,
98MR, 98MC, 98/99T, 100/101, 101L,
104, 108, 109, 111, 112/113, 115, 117L,
122, 122/123, 123L, 124, 124/125, 125L,
126, 127, 128L, 128/129, 129, 130, 131,
132, 133, 134, 135, 136, 137; Starwood
104/105; Tony Halliday/Apa Publications
15L, 31, 76, 91; Zeyrekhane Restaurant
116; Zuma Restaurant 113L
Cover credits: Front Cover Main: Blue
Mosque *Corbis* slippers *Getty*; Back Cover:
(Left) Ferry *Rebecca Erol/Apa* (Right): Galata
Tower *Rebecca Erol/Apa*

Printed by CTPS – China
© 2014 Apa Publications (UK) Ltd
All Rights Reserved

First Edition 2014

DISTRIBUTION

Worldwide
APA Publications GmbH & Co. Verlag KG
(Singapore branch)
7030 Ang Mo Kio Ave 5, 08-65
Northstar @ AMK, Singapore 569880
Email: apasin@singnet.com.sg
UK and Ireland
Dorling Kindersley Ltd
(a Penguin Group Company)
80 Strand, London, WC2R 0RL, UK
Email: sales@uk.dk.com
US
Ingram Publisher Services
One Ingram Blvd, PO Box 3006, La Vergne,
TN 37086-1986
Email: ips@ingramcontent.com
Australia
Universal Publishers
PO Box 307, St. Leonards NSW 1590
Email: sales@universalpublishers.com.au
New Zealand
Brown Knows Publications
11 Artesia Close, Shamrock Park, Auckland,
New Zealand 2016
Email: sales@brownknows.co.nz

INDEX

LEGEND

★ Place of interest
ⓘ Tourist information
Ⓜ Metro station
𝟏 Statue/monument
✉ Main post office
🚌 Main bus station
- - - Ferry route
—●— Tram line / station

	Park
	Important building
	Hotel
	Transport hub
	Bazaar / shop
	Pedestrian area
	Urban area